THEY FLEW HURRICANES

THEY FLEW HURRICANES

by

Adrian Stewart

Pen & Sword
AVIATION

First published in Great Britain in 2005 by
Pen & Sword Aviation
an imprint of
Pen & Sword Books Ltd
47 Church Street
Barnsley
South Yorkshire
S70 2AS

ISBN 1 84415 335 5

A CIP catalogue record for this book is
available from the British Library.

Typeset in Sabon by
Phoenix Typesetting, Auldgirth, Dumfriesshire

Printed and bound in England by
CPI UK

Pen & Sword Books Ltd incorporates the Imprints of Pen & Sword
Aviation, Pen & Sword Maritime, Pen & Sword Military, Wharncliffe
Local History, Pen & Sword Select, Pen & Sword Military Classics and
Leo Cooper.

For a complete list of Pen & Sword titles please contact
PEN & SWORD BOOKS LIMITED
47 Church Street, Barnsley, South Yorkshire, S70 2AS, England
E-mail: enquiries@pen-and-sword.co.uk
Website: www.pen-and-sword.co.uk

To the Hurricane pilots – of course

Contents

Preface

Once upon a time I wrote a book called *Hurricane*, which was subtitled *The War Exploits of the Fighter Aircraft* so as not to mislead anyone who wanted to read about a meteorological phenomenon. Since then much admirable research has been carried out by authors like Chaz Bowyer, Terence Kelly, Francis K. Mason, and particularly Christopher Shores and his changing band of associates. Were I to write the book now, I would correct some details and change the emphasis in certain cases, but I am pleased to say that I have seen nothing that alters my main conclusions, particularly my belief that the Hurricane's achievements were immense and have been persistently understated.

In order to demonstrate the Hurricane's importance, I described in some detail, not only its own activities but also the campaigns in which it fought. As it saw action in a wide variety of roles, in an extraordinary number of campaigns, pressure of space inevitably necessitated a limited treatment of certain other aspects of its career. One of these was its design and development but this omission gave me few qualms because, quite apart from the fact that I was more interested in what the Hurricane (and its pilots) did than in the precise speed or height at which it was flying at the time, the subject had and has been exhaustively covered elsewhere both before and since.

The other area in which I was restricted did, however, cause regrets. With a few notable exceptions such as *Fighter Pilot*, Wing Commander Paul Richey's splendid description of his experiences with 1 Squadron in France, there seemed to be little in the way of personal accounts of what the Hurricane was like in action.

Squadron diaries and pilots' combat reports filled part of the gap but they tend to be strictly factual as well as deliberately unemotional and restrained. Happily it is in just this field that recent studies have proved so valuable, making available a mass of additional records or reminiscences.

What follows therefore is the story of the Hurricane's war exploits from a different angle. It will cut down on detail, take most of the background for granted and do no more than mention some minor campaigns. Instead it will concentrate on the experiences of those who were involved with the Hurricane at the time. We shall hear from the design staff who created it, from the indispensable ground crews who kept it flying, from senior officers on both sides whose plans it helped to bring to fruition or to frustrate as the case might be, and from soldiers or seamen whom it supported or protected. But chiefly, as is only right, we shall hear from the pilots. For the Hurricane's achievements were their achievements, and without them it could have achieved nothing at all.

Acknowledgements

My grateful thanks are due:

For advice, encouragement and assistance in getting the book produced to: Bobby Gainher; Amy Myers; Bryan Watkins; Andrew Hewson, Elizabeth Fairbairn, Charlie Campbell and their colleagues at Johnson & Alcock Ltd; Brigadier Henry Wilson and his team at Pen & Sword Books Ltd.

For the photographs to: Terence Kelly; Christopher Shores; Philip Fisher and the staff of the Birmingham & Midland Institute & Library; the staff of the Taylor Library.

For permission to use extracts from the following books to: Air Research Publications for *Hurricane Squadron at War 1939–1941* by Perry Adams; Ian Allen Publishing for *Hurricane Special* by Maurice Allward; Crecy Publishing Ltd for *Pattle: Supreme Fighter in the Air* republished as *Pattle: Ace of Aces* by E.C.R. Baker; Pen & Sword Books Ltd for *The Desert Air War 1939–1945* by Richard Townshend Bickers; Chaz Bowyer for his *Hurricane at War*; The Crowood Press for *The Hawker Hurricane* by Peter Jacobs; Juliet Burton Literary Agency on behalf of the Author for *Hurricane and Spitfire Pilots at War* and *Hurricane Over the Jungle* by Terence Kelly; Crecy Publishing Ltd for *The Hawker Hurricane* by Francis K. Mason; Grub Street Publishing Ltd for *Air War for Yugoslavia, Greece and Crete 1940–41*, *Bloody Shambles* Volumes One and Two, *Malta: The Hurricane Years 1940–41* and *Malta: The Spitfire Year 1942* by Christopher Shores and others; Christopher Shores himself for the above plus

Fighters Over the Desert and *Fighters Over Tunisia*. Every effort has been made to trace copyright holders, as Andrew, Elizabeth and Charlie will confirm with some fervour, but if any have proved impossible to contact would they please accept my most sincere apologies.

Most of all, however, my thanks are due to the authors and publishers of the works from which the accounts of the pilots and others have been taken:

Adams, Perry, *Hurricane Squadron at War 1939–1941*, Air Research Publications, 1988.

Allward, Maurice, *Hurricane Special*, Ian Allen, 1975.

Bader, Group Captain Sir Douglas, *Fight for the Sky: The Story of the Spitfire and the Hurricane*, Sidgwick & Jackson, 1973.

Baker, E.C.R., *Pattle: Supreme Fighter in the Air*, Kimbers, 1965. Republished as *Pattle: Ace of Aces*, Crecy Publishing Ltd, 1993.

Barker, Ralph, *The Hurricats*, Pelham Books, 1978.

Beamont, Wing Commander Roland, *Phoenix into Ashes*, Kimbers, 1968.

Beedle, J., *43 Squadron*, Beaumont Aviation Literature, 1966.

Bickers, Richard Townshend, *The Desert Air War 1939–1945*, Leo Cooper, 1991.

——, *Ginger Lacey, Fighter Pilot*, Robert Hale, 1962.

Bolitho, Hector, *Combat Report*, Batsford, 1943.

Bowyer, Chaz, *Hurricane at War*, Ian Allen, 1974.

Cameron, Ian, *Red Duster, White Ensign*, Frederick Muller, 1959.

Clostermann, Pierre, *The Big Show*, Chatto & Windus, 1953.

Darlington, Roger, *Night Hawk*, Kimbers, 1985.

Dibbs, John & Holmes, Tony, *Hurricane: A Fighter Legend*, Osprey Publishing, 1995.

Donahue, Flight Lieutenant A.G., *Last Flight from Singapore*, MacMillan, 1944.

Forrester, Larry, *Fly for your Life*, Frederick Muller, 1956.

Fozard, Dr John W., *Sydney Camm and The Hurricane*, Airlife Publishing Ltd, 1991.

Gleed, Wing Commander I., *Arise to Conquer*, Victor Gollanz, 1942.

Halpenny, Bruce Barrymore, *Fight for the Sky: True Stories of Wartime Fighter Pilots*, Patrick Stephens, 1986.

Howell, Edward, *Escape to Live*, Longmans, 1950.

Jackson, Robert, *Hawker Hurricane*, Blandford Press, 1987.

Jacobs, Peter, *Hawker Hurricane*, Crowood Press, 1998.

Johnson, Brian, *Fly Navy*, David & Charles, 1981.

Kelly, Terence, *Hurricane and Spitfire Pilots at War*, Kimbers, 1986. Republished Arrow, 1988. Republished Pen & Sword Books Ltd, 2004.

——, *Hurricane Over the Jungle*, Kimbers 1977. Republished Pen & Sword Books Ltd, 2004.

Mason, Francis K., *The Hawker Hurricane*, Macdonalds, 1962. Republished in an extended version Aston Publications Ltd, 1987. Republished Crecy Publishing Ltd, 2001.

Masters, David, *So Few*, Eyre & Spottiswoode, 1943.

Moorehead, Alan, *The Desert War*, Hamish Hamilton, 1965.

Owen, Lieutenant Colonel Frank, *The Campaign in Burma*, HMSO, 1946.

Poolman, Kenneth, *Faith, Hope and Charity*, Kimbers, 1954.

Popham, Hugh, *Sea Flight*, Kimbers, 1954.

Richards, Denis & Saunders, Hilary St G., *Royal Air Force 1939–1945*, HMSO. Volume I: *The Fight at Odds*, 1953; Volume II: *The Fight Avails*, 1954; Volume III: *The Fight is Won*, 1954.

Richey, Wing Commander Paul, *Fighter Pilot*, Janes, 1980.

Robertson, Bruce & Scarborough Gerald, *Hawker Hurricane*, Patrick Stephens, 1974.

Shores, Christopher & Cull, Brian with Malizia, Nicola, *Air War for Yugoslavia, Greece and Crete 1940–41*, Grub Street Ltd, 1987.

——, *Malta: The Hurricane Years 1940–41*, Grub Street Ltd, 1987.

——, *Malta: The Spitfire Year 1942*, Grub Street Ltd, 1991.

Shores, Christopher & Cull, Brian with Izawa, Yasuho, *Bloody Shambles*, Grub Street Ltd. Volume One: *The Drift to War to the Fall of Singapore*, 1992; Volume Two: *The Defence of Sumatra to the Fall of Burma*, 1993.

Shores, Christopher & Ring, Hans, *Fighters Over the Desert*, Neville Spearman, 1969.

Shores, Christopher, Ring, Hans & Hess, William H., *Fighters Over Tunisia*, Neville Spearman, 1975.

Sims, Charles, *The Royal Air Force: The First Fifty Years*, Adam & Charles Black, 1968.

Swinson, Arthur, *Kohima*, Hutchinson, 1966.

Tomlinson, Michael, *The Most Dangerous Moment*, Kimbers, 1976.

Townsend, Group Captain Peter, *Duel of Eagles*, Weidenfeld & Nicolson, 1972.

Tsuji, Colonel Masanobu, *Singapore: The Japanese Version*, Mayflower-Dell, 1960 (UK Edition 1966).

And the following booklets prepared by the Ministry of Information for the Air Ministry:

The Air Battle of Malta, HMSO, 1944.
The Battle of Britain, HMSO, 1941.
Over to You, HMSO, 1943.

Chapter 1

Background

It all began with an entry in the project diary of an aircraft designer:

> August 1933. Meeting with Air Cdre [Commodore] Cave-Brown-Cave (Air Staff) and Major Buchanan (Deputy Director of Technical Development) to discuss possibility of building the Fury Monoplane, a single-seater fighter armed with two machine-guns in the fuselage and two in the wings.

The diary in question was that of Sydney Camm – he belatedly became Sir Sydney in 1953 – Chief Designer of Hawker Aircraft Limited, and the meeting to which he referred may be said to have marked the conception of the Hawker Hurricane. It had been inspired by two quite different yet interconnected series of events. One had begun in early 1930 with the introduction to squadron service in the RAF of an earlier creation by Camm, the Hawker Hart light bomber. With a top speed of 184 mph, this was faster than any existing RAF fighter and would prove to have a performance only marginally inferior to that of the two new fighters which would join the RAF in the following year, Camm's own Fury and Demon, the latter a two-seater fighter version of the Hart. Demands by the Air Ministry for a fighter with a clear dominance over the Hart would later lead to the Gloster Gladiator, but for his part Camm had become convinced that the biplane had reached its limit and a quite different solution to the problem was needed.

The other series of events had begun as recently as 30 January 1933 but had then moved with disconcerting rapidity. On that date Adolf Hitler had become Chancellor of Germany and his Air Minister, Hermann Göring, who was a great believer in putting 'guns before butter', promptly set in train a huge increase in aircraft production, backed by massive state loans, which was intended to give his Luftwaffe superiority over any possible rival.

In this anxious atmosphere, Camm's proposal for a 'Fury Monoplane' was accepted in principle forthwith. It was envisaged that the machine would have a closed cockpit, a fixed undercarriage and, as recorded in Camm's diary, four machine guns instead of the two that the Fury carried. Its engine would be a Rolls-Royce Goshawk which was also the powerplant of a later development of the Fury called the PV3. In reality numerous alterations were made during the design stage which resulted in the aircraft having a retractable undercarriage, a new Rolls-Royce engine, to become famous as the Merlin, and an armament of eight Browning 0·303-inch machine guns, though they were not carried when it first flew, ballast being placed in the wings to compensate.

All these changes meant that the connection with the Fury became rather remote and a new name had to be found for the aeroplane. It would of course ultimately be called the Hurricane but that was not until 27 June 1936; from early 1934 it was known simply as the 'Interceptor Monoplane'. In August it became the subject of Air Ministry Specification F36/34 which called for the production of a fighter with just those characteristics which it now possessed; this was followed by a contract for one prototype with the registered serial number K5083.

Meanwhile on 19 July, the then National government, alarmed by growing international tension, announced its aim of increasing the RAF by forty-one squadrons within five years. It was not a plan which met with universal approval, the Labour and Liberal parties forming a pact to defeat it, but on 30 July their motion of censure was defeated by 404 votes to 60. It is a terrifying thought that had the verdict gone the other way, Specification F36/34 would probably never have been issued. Nor for that matter would Specification F37/34 which brought about a similar order for a prototype from Supermarine, a firm which, as its name suggests, had specialized in high-speed seaplanes. Supermarine's fighter, to which was given the arresting name of 'Spitfire', was of a more modern design than the Hurricane. This would result in a higher performance but also in considerable delays during its early development while numerous problems were ironed out. Sydney Camm's philosophy was different, as is related by Philip Lucas, one of Hawkers' test pilots:[1]

I should point out now, that all through the design study stages Hawkers knew that they would be up against very stiff competition from Supermarine who had the benefit of long design experience with their metal-skinned Schneider Trophy monoplane racers. Obviously they would apply that knowledge and go all out for the fastest possible fighter. With no background experience in designing high-speed monoplanes nor in stressed-skin wings or monocoque fuselages, Hawkers knew that their best chances in winning a production order lay in producing a design which, whilst meeting the performance required, would be quick and easy to produce.

The system of production adopted therefore was basically the same as that developed for the Hart and Fury biplane series. This had been proved over the previous six years to be robust, simple to manufacture and, even more important, easy to repair. As events turned out, Sydney Camm's decision to adopt a system which was well within the existing know-how of both the design and production facilities at Kingston, was an extremely wise one. In my opinion it was the key to the Hurricane's success. Had he attempted to compete with Supermarine in building the fastest possible fighter, as opposed to the most practical and easy to produce, there can be little doubt the Royal Air Force would not have had a single modern fighter to send to France when the war broke out. Neither would they have been able to cover the British Army's withdrawal from Dunkirk, and almost certainly we would have lost the Battle of Britain. This is no overstatement. There just would not have been enough fighters.

Happily Camm did concentrate on ease of production. By 1939 Hurricanes would be pouring off the production lines at Kingston, at Brooklands, at Hawkers' new factory at Langley – built for the express purpose of producing Hurricanes – and at the Hucclecote factory of Gloster Aircraft Company which had become a subsidiary of Hawkers in 1934. Moreover in early 1940, Hurricanes would begin to reach Britain from the Canadian Car & Foundry Co Ltd of Montreal, to which Hawkers had supplied full details of every Hurricane component on microfilm.

With ease of production the Hurricane combined ease of maintenance, a virtue blessed by the RAF's loyal, skilful ground crews, whose efforts have received little recognition but were of vital importance, fully appreciated at least by their pilots. The Hurricane's 'old-fashioned' construction meant that ground personnel found it very little different from the biplanes they had previously tended. This not only contributed to the speed with which it was incorporated into the RAF but helped to ensure that throughout its career, and despite having to operate in some singularly unpleasant locations, a greater percentage of Hurricanes could be kept serviceable than was the case with any other type of aircraft.

As the war continued, another advantage of the Hurricane's simple design would become increasingly apparent. One of those who experienced this was Frank Hartley, a member of No. 2 R & R (Refuelling and Rearming) Party which was stationed at Manston, Kent to service visiting aircraft using this advanced base when embarking on or returning from raids across the Channel. In Chaz Bowyer's *Hurricane at War*, he describes how:

> Perhaps one of the greatest attributes of the Hurricane lay in its capacity to absorb punishment and still fly. The fuselage aft of the cockpit was fabric-covered and it was not unusual to find bullet or shrapnel holes in this area, which could easily be repaired providing that the interior airframe structure and equipment were undamaged. Similar damage to a stressed-skin (ie metal-covered) aircraft, such as the Spitfire, needed more time to effect a suitable repair. I have a vivid recollection of one Hurricane landing with tail planes, elevators and

4

rudder reduced to a mere framework, with pieces of fabric hanging loose. As we surveyed the damage I remember thinking that this kite had defied all the known laws of aerodynamics as its pilot had coaxed it home.

Since we have now recorded a couple of comparisons with the Spitfire, it may be as well to make some others at this stage. This is not done to denigrate in any way the most beautiful, graceful and elegant aeroplane of the Second World War, but to correct the misconceptions which since that time have arisen over the role of its less glamorous but, in the first part of the conflict, more important partner.

The Spitfire was faster than the Hurricane with a better rate of climb. It was also capable of considerable development, as a result of which it remained as a front-line fighter pure and simple throughout the war while more and more powerful engines were put into its nose; in fact many of the later versions were so different from the original that a change of name was seriously contemplated. The Hurricane on the other hand had ceased to be employed on front-line fighter duties in Britain by the end of 1941 and overseas some eighteen months later – though its versatility ensured that it remained in action on other tasks until the end of hostilities. It must be emphasized, however, that during the crucial early years the Hurricane was in no way a 'poor relation'. On the contrary, it was then in many respects a much more practical warplane than the Spitfire; a verdict reached not just by devoted Hurricane pilots but by those who had gained experience on both types or had even converted from Spitfires.

One of these was Wing Commander Robert Stanford Tuck. He had flown Spitfires with 65 and 92 Squadrons but was given command of a Hurricane squadron, No. 257, towards the end of the Battle of Britain. His biographer Larry Forrester in *Fly for your Life*, quotes Tuck as declaring:

My first reaction wasn't good. After the Spit, she [the Hurricane] was like a flying brick – a great, lumbering farmyard stallion compared with a dainty and gentle thoroughbred. The Spit was so much smaller, sleeker,

5

smoother – and a bit faster too. It nearly broke my heart, because things seemed tough enough without having to take on 109s in a heavy great kite like this.

But after the first few minutes I began to realize the Hurri had virtues of her own. She was solid, obviously able to stand up to an awful lot of punishment . . . steady as a rock – a wonderful gun platform . . . just as well powered as any other fighter in the world, with the same Merlin I knew and trusted so well.

The pilot's visibility was considerably better than in the Spit, because the nose sloped downwards more steeply from the cockpit to the spinner. This, of course, gave much better shooting conditions. The undercart was wider and, I think, stronger than the Spit's. This made landing a lot less tricky, particularly on rough ground. The controls were much heavier and it took a lot more muscle to haul her around the sky – and yet, you know, after that first hop, after I'd got the feel of her, I never seemed to notice this, or any of the other differences any more.

Group Captain Sir Douglas Bader had an even higher opinion of the Hurricane. He first saw service with No. 19 and 222 (Spitfire) Squadrons but during the Battle of Britain he commanded a Hurricane squadron, No. 242, and also a unit consisting of two Spitfire and three Hurricane squadrons (including 242) known as the 12 Group Wing. In his book *Fight for the Sky: The Story of the Spitfire and the Hurricane,* he states emphatically that:

Like all pilots who flew and fought in the Hurricane I, I grew to love it. It was strong, highly manoeuvrable, could turn inside the Spitfire and of course the Me 109. Best of all, it was a marvellous gun platform. The sloping nose gave you a splendid forward view, while the eight guns were set in blocks of four in each wing, close to the fuselage. The aeroplane remained rock steady when you fired. Unlike the Spitfire with its lovely elliptical wing which sloped upwards to the tip, the Hurricane wing was thicker and straight. The Spitfire was less steady when the guns were firing because, I have always thought, they were spread further along the wing, and the recoil effect was noticeable.

Similar comments are made by Major James Goodson in Terence Kelly's *Hurricane and Spitfire Pilots at War*:[2]

The Hurricane was a much better gun platform. Of course you know the difference in performance, but when it came to *shooting* from a Hurricane, number one, if you were in a turn . . . [its] nose didn't blank you out. Because to get enough deflection in a very tight turn with a Spit, the nose would blank out the target. And the Hurricane was so stable . . . The first few attacks I made [in a] Spitfire [it] was jumping around such a lot. And if you got in the other fellow's slipstream, you had a terrible time. And I missed three of four victories which should have been a cinch simply because the Spitfire was bouncing around . . . But then of course, when you'd got used to it, it was all right! Everybody loved the Spit. The Hurricane was an old workhorse if you like, and I loved it and it was a good gun platform and at the right altitude it was more manoeuvrable. Of course the Luftwaffe, when you talk to the Luftwaffe boys, they had more respect for the Spitfire than they had for the Hurricane because the Spitfire could catch them, but they never mixed with either of them in a dogfight. In a dogfight the Hurricane was every bit as good as the Spitfire. It was a great plane. I loved the Hurricane. You know what George Bulman, Hawkers' chief test pilot, said of the Hurricane first time he saw it: 'Well it may not fly but it certainly won't break!'

Goodson's remarks about the Luftwaffe are very relevant, for the unfairly dismissive attitude adopted by some commentators towards the Hurricane stems from that of its former foes. Ridiculous as it seems, they actually preferred to be shot down by Spitfires. On 8 April 1940 for instance, a Hurricane pilot of 43 Squadron, Flight Lieutenant – later Group Captain – Peter Townsend returned to his base at Wick to view a fascinating scene. He describes it in his book *Duel of Eagles*:

In the middle of the airfield lay a Heinkel He 111, wheels up, propellers bent. Apparently [Sergeant] Hallowes had hit it and the pilot had turned back to the coast. Mistaking our flare path for lights on the sea he decided to 'ditch'. Before the astonished eye of the airfield control officer the Heinkel ground to a standstill. A door was opened, a dinghy thrown out and two of the crew – bootless, for easier swimming – dived out onto dry land. Rumour even had it that they climbed into their dinghy and began rowing.

Later they insisted that a Spitfire had attacked them. It was the first sign of the Luftwaffe's 'Spitfire snobbery'. There were no Spitfires within miles.

Such an attitude becomes the more absurd when it is appreciated that the general standard of aircraft recognition in the Luftwaffe was surprisingly poor for such a very efficient service. In North Africa the Germans confused Hurricanes, Tomahawks and Kittyhawks almost as a matter of routine. Nor was their record much better in North-Western Europe, for there the issue was further clouded by their 'Spitfire snobbery'. As Townsend points out:

The Jäger [fighter pilots] of the Luftwaffe did not think the Hurricane was much good. This may have been partly because they often mistook Hurricanes for Spitfires. Both Kesselring [head of Luftflotte – Air Fleet – 2 in the Battle of France and Battle of Britain] and Osterkamp [his fighter commander] fell into the trap. 'Uncle Theo' 'saw' Spitfires on the ground in the Battle of France; Kesselring said, 'Only the Spitfires worried us.' Both were wrong. There were no Spitfires in France and in the Battle of Britain they shot down, in the aggregate, fewer than the Hurricanes.

To which it need only be added that the Germans and their Italian allies would later detect Spitfires in the Balkans or the Middle East at a time when the nearest one was several hundred miles away. A few – in fairness a very few – Japanese airmen would go still further, reporting that they had sighted Spitfires when the nearest one was several thousand miles away. Whatever Shakespeare's Juliet may have said, there is a very great deal in a wonderfully evocative name.

Not of course that the enemy's misconceptions really mattered in any case. What was important was the attitude of the Hurricanes' own pilots and, as we have already seen, they were delighted with the quality of their 'mounts'. This was singularly fortunate, because they would soon be called on to accept awesome responsibilities.

NOTES

1 *A Hurricane History* by Philip G. Lucas GM, FRAeS. This was a lecture originally given by Mr Lucas to the Hatfield Branch of the Royal Aeronautical Society. It is repeated as a chapter in *Sydney Camm and the Hurricane: Perspectives on the Master Fighter Designer and his Finest Achievement* by Dr John W. Fozard. Dr Fozard was a member of Camm's design team as from 1950 and later Chief Designer of the Harrier.
2 Goodson was an American citizen who had entered the RAF as a volunteer. He later rejoined his own country's armed forces when the RAF Eagle squadrons were formed into the Fourth Fighter Group of the US Army Air Force, the pilots replacing their RAF ranks with the equivalent American ones.

Chapter 2

Early Encounters

First of all the Hurricane pilots was P.W.S. 'George' Bulman, chief test pilot of Hawker Aircraft Limited, who on 6 November 1935 took off from Brooklands aerodrome, by the famous motor-racing track, on the maiden flight of the Hurricane prototype K5083. His colleague Philip Lucas tells us that:

> The first flight was quite uneventful, being done with the undercarriage down, and I well remember our surprise at the low approach speed and short landing run of that first flight. I think too, that Bulman was quite astonished. We had not experienced before the combined lift effect of a thick wing section and the ground cushion provided by a low wing monoplane. Later, when we learned that the use of the engine was a 'must' for normal approach and landing, particularly as weight and wing loading increased, we began to appreciate the startling increase in lift which could be obtained by making use of the propeller slip-stream effect with varying degrees of throttle settings.
>
> This characteristic, coupled with the very wide-track undercarriage, was the main reason why average squadron pilots found it so easy to convert to Hurricanes from their previous biplanes and, more importantly, why the accident rate in service was so much lower than anticipated.
>
> We found the aeroplane easy to fly, stable in flight and on the ground and with a much better view than anything we

had flown before . . . [In view of this judgement and the RAF's urgent need for modern fighters] the prototype K5083 was flown to [the Aircraft and Armament Experimental Establishment at] Martlesham Heath on 7 February 1936, after only ten flights totalling 8 hours and 5 minutes in the air. Fortunately for everybody, the Martlesham pilots' first impressions were as favourable as ours. They reported on the aircraft's remarkable ease of handling and its excellent control at all speeds down to the stall. Its comparatively low approach and landing speed was particularly noted, and all this with an in-flight performance greater than ever before experienced . . . The only thing which marred the otherwise very satisfactory trial was the continued unreliability of the engine.

Despite the problems with the Merlin engine and although only one machine had so far flown, belief in the new fighter was in fact widespread. On 3 June 1936 the Air Ministry approved a contract for 600 of them – the largest order yet placed for a military aircraft in peacetime. Hawkers' own confidence was even higher, for in March, without even awaiting the anticipated contract, the Company had instructed its planning department to commence schedules catering for the production of 1,000 aeroplanes. It was a superb illustration of private enterprise – in every sense of the word – but Hawkers were certain that export orders would cover any excess over RAF requirements. If there were any doubters, their fears would be calmed on 1 November 1938 when the Air Ministry issued a contract for a further 1,000 Hurricanes.

Certainly the prototype's performance gave good grounds for confidence. It had a speed of 318 mph at 15,500 feet, being the first interceptor in Britain, or indeed the world, to exceed 300 mph. It could climb to 15,000 feet in 5.7 minutes; to 20,000 feet in 8.4 minutes. Service ceiling was 34,500 feet and estimated absolute ceiling 35,400 feet. Moreover when the first Hurricane Mark I, L1547, took off from Brooklands on its maiden flight on 12 October 1937, with Lucas at the controls, it had a performance which was already slightly superior as a result of lessons learned on the prototype and which would continue to improve as later modifications were introduced. It also carried eight 0.303-inch Browning machine guns.

Nonetheless the difficulties with the engine did have the adverse effect of checking, initially at least, Hawkers' ability to mass-produce its Hurricanes with the minimum of delay. K5083 had flown with a variety of early Merlins, but by September 1936 it was decided that the RAF aircraft would carry the Merlin G – or Merlin II as it was also called – driving a two-bladed, fixed-pitch, wooden propeller. This necessitated the alteration of the Hurricane's nose, air-intake, engine cowlings, engine mounting, glycol tank and hand starting system. As a result, it was not until December 1937 that Hurricanes first began to appear on a fighter squadron, No. 111, stationed at Northolt.

By the time of the Munich crisis in September 1938 the RAF had four squadrons equipped with modern fighters – all of them with Hurricanes. Of these, 73 and 87 Squadrons were not fully operational, while the Hurricanes of 111 and 56 Squadrons could not fight at over 15,000 feet as they then lacked heating for their gun-bays. By contrast, the Luftwaffe already possessed a powerful bomber force with the priceless practical experience gained by the Condor Legion in the Spanish Civil War. Had hostilities commenced at that time, the citizens of Britain might well have endured a number of very unpleasant experiences. Possibly realization of this acted as a spur; in any case shortly thereafter the flow of Hurricanes to Fighter Command became a flood.

The date was 24 September 1938. The place was RAF Biggin Hill. My excitement was intense for today I was to fly Hurricane L1655, the first of No. 32 Sqn's long-awaited replacements for our Gloster Gauntlet biplanes.

Having studied Pilot's Notes I climbed into the cockpit and sat for a while finding my way around the levers and switches, then started up and taxied over the grass – we had no runways – to the boundary, and took off. The big two-bladed wooden propeller gave surprisingly rapid acceleration, whilst the throaty roar of the Merlin and the solid, rugged, feel of the aircraft as it bounded over the uneven surface stimulated and inspired confidence.

12

Retracting the wheels, a novel experience, involved moving the left hand from throttle to stick and select[ing] wheels up with the right hand and depressing the pump-lever until the wheels locked up. As this loss of throttle control made formation take-offs unusually interesting we later surreptitiously attached a Bowden cable from the stick to the lever to avoid the hand change. Now airborne, I closed the canopy, another novel experience, and relieved of the head-buffeting slipstream of an open cockpit, settled down to enjoy myself.

Having climbed to a safe height, I tried a variety of aerobatics and was delighted by the immediate and smooth response to the controls. When stalling the aircraft I was interested to note that the right wing dropped, a Sydney Camm characteristic I had found common in other aircraft he had designed. On landing from this 50-minute 'Type experience' flight I looked forward with exultation to the future, and the opportunity to get to know the Hurricane really well.

Such were the reactions of the future Air Commodore Peter Brothers, as he describes them in *Hurricane: A Fighter Legend* by John Dibbs and Tony Holmes, but not all new Hurricane pilots felt a similar emotion. No. 1 Squadron at the time of Munich had been flying Hawker Fury biplanes and the CO had warned his pilots that the only way these were likely to destroy enemy bombers was by ramming them. It might have been thought therefore that they would have welcomed their Furies' more modern successors. In fact many had their doubts, including a young sergeant pilot attached to the squadron from the Volunteer Reserve, who was later to make a name for himself but who now believed that he:

would never be able to fly one. Sergeant 'Lofty' Luckham, however, who had qualified on these strange beasts, soon dispelled this lack of confidence with some encouraging words . . . 'Don't touch that lever in the right hand corner of the cockpit there, while you're on the ground, or the aeroplane will fall down. Otherwise, she's exactly the same as a

Fury.' . . . I didn't touch the lever in the right hand corner, while on the ground; or in the air; nor, I must admit, did I touch it for the next two flights either: I had no confidence whatsoever in retractable undercarriages at that time and wasn't sure that the wheels would ever come down again.

This account by Squadron Leader James Lacey, quoted in *Ginger Lacey: Fighter Pilot* by Richard Townshend Bickers, gives only one reason why some of the early Hurricane pilots left the under-carriage down in flight. Many preferred to do so because they found the aircraft's speed with the undercarriage raised frighten-ingly fast. This may seem astonishing when the performance of later aircraft is considered, but it must be remembered that almost all the pilots had been used to biplanes, with a top wing above them and an open cockpit. Flying a low-wing monoplane with a closed cockpit seemed an entirely different proposition, especially as there was then an unjustified belief that monoplanes lacked structural integrity.

Fortunately, practical experience soon convinced the airmen that their new mounts were robust, reliable and completely free from any vice. That the Hurricane quickly became a familiar sight throughout Fighter Command undoubtedly helped – though in this instance familiarity brought with it not contempt but respect and affection. Unwisely, as it might seem in retrospect, a number of Hurricanes were exported to Canada, South Africa, Yugoslavia, Belgium, Turkey, Rumania, Persia and Poland – and later, it may be mentioned in passing, to Finland, Portugal and Eire – but there were still 497 Hurricanes in service with seventeen squadrons or in reserve when, on 3 September 1939, the Second World War began.

Quality increased as well as quantity. Metal wings for example replaced those previously covered with fabric. The old wooden propeller, which had a tendency to fly into pieces under stress, was replaced by a De Havilland metal, three-bladed, two-pitch propeller. With this the pilot could alter the pitch – ie the angle – of the blades so as to use fine (low) pitch for take-off and coarse (high) pitch for greater speeds – much as gears are used in a car. This ensured not only fuel economy but an improvement in rate of climb. Later Rolls-Royce brought about a further advance by designing the Merlin III engine, driving a Rotol constant-speed propeller, which adjusted the pitch to the engine speed. Earlier machines were subsequently brought up to these improved standards, most of them being converted by early 1940, though even in August of that year there were still a handful in service with fabric-covered wings or wooden propellers or both.

Though the aircraft's weight was increased by the installation of armour plate to provide added protection for the pilot, the Hurricane Mark I could still show a superior speed to that of the prototype. It could in fact attain 320–328 mph, the variation depending on the degree of skill in the finishing shops of different factories.

Certainly the pilots of No. 1 Squadron had long since lost their initial reservations when, on the outbreak of war, four Hurricane squadrons were dispatched to France. Nos. 85 and 87 Squadrons were stationed in north-eastern France, where they formed the fighter portion of the Air Component which supported the British Expeditionary Force, but No. 1 Squadron, together with 73 Squadron, moved to Lorraine behind the Maginot Line. Here they were intended to give protection to the Advanced Air Striking Force, a body of twelve Battle or Blenheim bomber squadrons detailed for attacks or reconnaissance across the German frontier. In reality their Hurricanes, and indeed those in the Air Component as well, spent most of their time dealing with enemy aircraft crossing the French frontier. Flying Officer – later Wing Commander – Paul Richey describes No. 1 Squadron's initial encounter with the Luftwaffe in his *Fighter Pilot*:[1]

Our first victory was on 30 October 1939 – a gloriously sunny day with no low cloud but quite a lot of high wispy stuff. I was on the airfield [Vassincourt] by my machine when we heard unfamiliar aircraft engines. After a lot of neck-craning and squinting we saw it – a Dornier Do 17 immediately above us at some 20,000 feet, travelling west and just visible in the thinner clouds. Like all Luftwaffe aircraft it was light-blue underneath and difficult to spot. The French ack-ack opened up but got nowhere near it.

This was the first Hun we'd seen, and we were wildly

excited. [Sergeant] Soper and I rushed off in pursuit, but had to watch our take-off and lost him. We saw him again from 3,000 feet, but lost him soon after. Up and up we climbed, turning gently from side to side and straining our eyes to find him. We didn't and . . . came down after fifteen minutes' search.

[The pilots had returned to their airfield when] a Hurricane dived across rocking its wings, turned, came back and repeated the performance, obviously highly excited. It was [Pilot Officer] 'Boy' Mould, who had joined the Squadron in June. He had just finished re-fuelling after a patrol when the same Dornier went over. He took off without waiting for orders, pulled his plug (boost-override), lost the Hun, climbed up to 18,000 feet – and found him. He did an ordinary straight astern attack, firing one longish burst with his sights starting above the Dornier and moving slowly round the fuselage. The Hun caught fire immediately, went into a vertical spiral and made a whopping hole in the French countryside: it exploded on striking the ground.

Five hands was all that remained of the crew of four, but four coffins were given a funeral with military honours at which the Squadron was represented. We were all pleased at our first success, but we were sorry for the poor devils we had killed. 'Boy' got very drunk that night and confided to me, 'I'm bloody sorry I went and looked at the wreck. What gets me down is the thought that *I* did it!'

It should be added that the reason why Hurricanes had been chosen for France was that they were already renowned for their reliability. Moreover those strong, wide undercarriages were rightly considered suitable for every conceivable form of landing surface. This perhaps was just as well, judging from the account by Reg Guppy, a member of the ground crew, which appears in *Hurricane Squadron: No 87 Squadron at War 1939–1941* by Perry Adams:

During the months that we were in France we were to experience all types of weather, from sunny and warm to the

16

other extreme of ice and snow, but the conditions that I remember the best were the mud and water-logged airfields. Here not only was refuelling a problem but every aspect of aircraft handling was one hard slog; it was common to have to literally lift the aircraft up on the backs of the erks underneath the wings to get the kites even to taxi in the mud. It was a common sight to see kites taking off more like speed-boats than aircraft . . . I am quite satisfied that no other fighter before or since would have put up with the treatment that the Hurricane endured in France in 1939 and 1940.

Of course its ruggedness also served the Hurricane well in combat as Paul Richey relates. On 23 November 1939, a section of No. 1 Squadron engaged a Heinkel He 111:

It was on fire, losing height rapidly, when a bunch of French Moranes came rushing in, all so eager to have a bang that one of them knocked most of Sergeant Clowes' tail off and the pilot had to bale out! Clowes put up a very good show getting his machine back to the airfield, though he had to land at 120 mph to keep control: he overshot and nosed over. I saw him straight after this little effort and, though he was laughing, he was trembling violently and couldn't talk coherently. I had a good look at his aircraft too: one elevator and half the rudder were completely gone.

This ruggedness was to prove of even greater value when the Hurricanes met enemy fighters. These were the single-engined Messerschmitt Bf 109 and the twin-engined Messerschmitt Bf 110. 'Bf' incidentally was short for 'Bayerische Flugzeugwerke' – Bavarian Aircraft Company. The abbreviation 'Me' was not officially correct until 1944, though it is used so consistently by RAF pilots that it would be pedantic to keep on correcting them. The 110 had a high reputation at this stage of the war which subsequent events were to disprove, but the 109 was undoubtedly a formidable opponent. Later suggestions that Hurricane pilots suffered an inferiority complex when facing it are, however, unsupported by those best qualified to judge. For example, Wing

Commander Roland Beamont, then a Pilot Officer in 87 Squadron, has this to say:

> In 1940 we used to hear a great deal about the superiority of the Me 109, which was a bit faster. And that's all it was, just a bit faster! . . . [On the other hand] the Hurricane could outmanoeuvre any aeroplane it met at that time. It could easily outmanoeuvre the Me 109.[2]

Paul Richey gives this account:

> At last on 29 March [1940] 1 Squadron met the German fighters . . . [Getting on the tail of a 109] I let him have it. My gun-button was sticking and I wasted ammunition, but he started to stream smoke. The pilot must have been hit, for he took no evasive action, merely falling slowly in a vertical spiral. I was very excited and dived on top of him using my remaining ammunition.[3] I then pulled out and saw another 109 about 2,000 feet above me. He headed for me, but knowing his speed to be superior I didn't dive away but turned on him, partly to stop him getting on my tail, and partly to bluff him. Either he had finished his hardware (which was unlikely, for the Germans carried 1,000 rounds for each gun to our 300) or he'd witnessed his chum's fate and wasn't feeling so brave. Anyway he beat it – and so did I at ground level.

During April, 1 Squadron destroyed five more 109s for the loss of one Hurricane, the pilot of which escaped by parachute. No. 73 Squadron's first encounter with enemy fighters had been less satisfactory. On 22 December 1939 three of its pilots were attacked from above by four 109s which shot down two of them, killing the pilots, both of whom had just come out from Britain, while losing only one of their own number destroyed and one damaged in the process. On 2 March 1940, however, Flying Officer Edgar 'Cobber' Kain – who was not an Australian but a New Zealander – destroyed a 109 and damaged two more before crash-landing his badly damaged Hurricane; and on the 26th he destroyed another pair of 109s before baling out of his blazing aircraft with a wounded leg. On the 26th also, another of 73 Squadron's airmen, Flying Officer Newell 'Fanny' Orton, shot down two further 109s, after which he landed safely. Both pilots were awarded the Distinguished Flying Cross.

The Hurricane pilots based in Britain did not have to bother with enemy fighters: their encounters were with bombers or reconnaissance aircraft. On 3 February 1940 Flight Lieutenant Peter Townsend attacked a Heinkel He 111 which crashed near Whitby, Yorkshire with two dead crewmen on board; this was the first hostile aircraft to be brought down on English (as distinct from Scottish) soil. Most of 43 Squadron's victims though, fell in the sea, which the airmen of both sides feared and hated far more than they did their human foes. On 22 February, for instance, as he records in *Duel of Eagles*, Townsend took another He 111 by surprise:

> The effect of my guns was devastating. The bomber staggered, emitting a cloud of oily vapour which obscured my windscreen. Then, as if the pilot had collapsed over the controls, it tipped into a steep dive at a terrifying speed. Suddenly both wings were wrenched off with fearful violence and the dismembered fuselage plummeted straight into the sea, followed by a trail of fluttering debris. Only at that moment did I realize what I had done to the men inside. I felt utterly nauseated.

In a later action, Townsend's Hurricane was among seven from 43 Squadron which combined against a single wretched Heinkel:

> As I came in I could see the tail unit was already wobbling and the engines streaming vapour. I turned aside and as the Heinkel glided down I flew in very close alongside it. [Flight Lieutenant] Caesar Hull stationed himself on the other side. The rear cockpit bore the signs of a charnel house with the gunner slumped inside it mutilated beyond recognition. His fair hair streaming in the slipstream which rushed through his shattered windscreen, the young pilot bent over the controls

19

trying to urge his stricken machine to fly. Through the window panels the two other members of the crew regarded me in silent despair. I pushed back my hood and signalled them to turn towards the coast. Those men were no longer enemies but airmen in distress. If only we could have borne up their doomed aircraft with our own wings. I knew I was watching the last moments of three brave men as they went down to perish in the sea. I watched the Heinkel until, unable to fly any more, it alighted awkwardly on the sea. The fuselage broke in half. One wing tipped crazily in the air then slithered under the surface. As I circled low overhead I could see the three men in yellow life-saving jackets struggling free and beginning to swim. Like some of the others I called base to fix our position and ask for help. We were some twenty miles from the coast. The three Germans would be dead long before help could reach them.

This incident occurred on 10 April. On the previous day German forces had swallowed up Denmark and launched a series of audacious invasions of Norway by sea and air. Occupation of this country would provide bases for flanking attacks on Britain, secure Germany's supply of Swedish iron ore which passed through the ice-free port of Narvik and, in the long term, threaten Britain's communications with Russia, then Hitler's ally and his partner in the brutal partition of Poland – but marked in the Führer's mind for ultimate destruction so as to achieve his aim of obtaining *Lebensraum*. Counter-moves by the British and French proved woefully inadequate and by mid-May the Germans were in full control of the whole of Norway except for the far north; even here an isolated German garrison, though heavily outnumbered by Allied troops who had landed at nearby Harstad, was still holding out in Narvik.

Since the Luftwaffe was now starting to dominate in the Narvik area as well, it was rightly considered that the Allied attack on this port must have fighter cover. To assist in providing it, the Hurricanes of 46 Squadron were hoisted on board the aircraft carrier HMS *Glorious* in somewhat undignified fashion, and on 26 May flew off her decks; after a proposed base at Skaanland had

20

proved unsuitable they went on to Bardufoss, an inconvenient 50 miles north of the ground forces they were supposed to protect. Here they joined 263 Squadron, equipped with Gladiator biplanes.

No. 46 was a very experienced squadron which on 21 October 1939 had made the first Hurricane 'kills' of the war by shooting down three Heinkel He 115 seaplanes and forcing a fourth to 'ditch'. Curiously enough, the squadron's first successes in Norway were also against enemy flying-boats. On 28 May they destroyed two Dornier Do 26s which were disembarking re-inforcements, even though these were moored under a cliff in a very narrow part of a fiord.

On the same day 46 Squadron's Hurricanes covered the Allied capture of Narvik and gained their first victory in the air when Flying Officer Lydall shot down a Junkers Ju 88. They saw further action on the 29th, as witness this report by Patric Jameson, their New Zealand-born senior Flight Lieutenant, in *So Few: The Immortal Record of the Royal Air Force* by David Masters:

There were three enemy aircraft flying in line astern at 10,000 feet, with half a mile between each. The leader was a Heinkel He 111 and the others were Junkers Ju 88s . . . I went up to attack the rear Junkers. I closed to 150 yards, and at my very first burst there was a terrific flash and my windscreen was obscured with oil and glycol. I broke away and circled above for a few seconds, and saw that his starboard propeller was stopping and his engine smoking. I went in again to give him another long burst, and as I was about to open fire he dropped his bombs and turned away south. I saw his starboard petrol tank between the engine and fuselage burst into flames and followed him down. Just before he crashed on top of a cliff, one of the crew baled out and alighted in the fiord – I don't know what happened to him.

Sadly events on other fronts had already ensured that the Allied occupation of Narvik would be of short duration. After demolishing the port installations and industrial plant – though ironically less thoroughly than the Germans had already done prior to their retirement – the troops there prepared to disembark. The evacuation lasted over five days commencing on 3 June, under the protection provided by the Hurricanes and Gladiators; this was so effective that the enemy did not realize until too late that a withdrawal was taking place. On 7 June 46 Squadron fought its final action in Norway, destroying a Heinkel He 111 and damaging another which crash-landed at its base. The last men to leave next day were the ground staff and some spare pilots who sailed on the merchantman *Arandora Star*.

Meanwhile on the 7th, the Gladiators flew off to join HMS *Glorious*, their low landing speed enabling them to do so without too much difficulty even though they lacked arrester hooks to catch the wires stretched over the carrier's flight deck. For the Hurricanes, much faster, and with a longer landing run, it was a different story. The basic problem was that the pilots would have to brake so hard to reduce their speed that it would be impossible for them to keep their aircrafts' tails down. If the Hurricanes did not nose over completely, they would never come to a halt but would simply run off the end of the deck. Accordingly, orders were sent to 46 Squadron's CO, Squadron Leader Kenneth Cross, to destroy his Hurricanes, now reduced by combat or accidents to ten in number, at their airfield.

The orders were not carried out. Knowing that Fighter Command needed every available Hurricane, Cross pleaded that he be allowed to risk a landing on the carrier. The senior RAF officer in Norway, Group Captain Moore, with considerable moral courage, took the responsibility of granting permission. Extra weight – specifically provided by bags of sand – was added to the tail sections of the Hurricanes' fuselages to help hold them down, and Cross called for volunteers to fly these unbalanced aeroplanes out to the *Glorious*. Every man in the squadron stepped forward.

As a slight concession to the risks involved, it was decided to have a limited trial run. Three aircraft only would make the first attempt. The remaining seven would await news from them before following.

At 1800 hrs Flt Lt Jameson, Fg Off Knight and Sgt Taylor took off for HMS *Glorious*. (46 Squadron Diary)

They reached the carrier after an hour's flight. Jameson, throttled back and flying at just above stalling speed, went in to land first. There was no bounce from the weighted tail when he touched down and the Hurricane rolled safely to a halt. Knight and Taylor successfully followed his example. Confirmation of the success was sent at once, but in the high, iron-bound Norwegian mountains, radio communications were very poor and it seems that the signal was not received. It made no difference; one feels that having gone this far nothing was going to stop Cross from making his attempt.

8th June 1940. 0045 hrs.[4] Sqn Ldr Cross, Flt Lt Stewart, Fg Offs Cowles, Frost and Mee, Plt Off Bunker and F/Sgt Shackley took off for HMS *Glorious*. (46 Squadron Diary)

All seven Hurricanes landed safely.

Sheer tragedy struck that afternoon. The German battle-cruisers *Scharnhorst* and *Gneisenau*, hunting for ships retiring from Norway, came upon *Glorious*. Their first hurried salvos, though fired at long range, struck home. The carrier's escorting destroyers *Ardent* and *Acasta* defended her nobly, the latter getting a torpedo into *Scharnhorst* before both were sunk – but their task was a hopeless one. The *Glorious*, burning furiously, went down some two hours after first being hit. Among over 1,100 men who were lost with her were eight Hurricane pilots. The only survivors were the future Air Commodore Patric Jameson and the future Air Chief Marshal Sir Kenneth Cross.

All ten Hurricanes were lost also. Their destruction passed unnoticed amidst the catastrophes which were elsewhere engulfing the RAF – and indeed the Allied cause in general.

NOTES
1 This book was derived from the very full diary that Richey kept at the time.
2 Quoted in *Sydney Camm and the Hurricane* by Dr John W. Fozard.
3 Enemy records show that Richey's 109 crash-landed with a wounded pilot at the controls.
4 0045 was daylight in the land of the midnight sun.

Chapter 3

Days of Disaster

One result of the earlier mishaps in Norway was a loss of confidence in Prime Minister Neville Chamberlain and his consequent replacement by Winston Churchill. There was a certain irony in this since Churchill, as First Lord of the Admiralty, bore most of the responsibility for those mishaps, but he was the one politician under whom all members of parliament were willing to serve, including his unselfish predecessor. Churchill took office on 10 May 1940 and by a still greater irony that day saw the start of a whole series of disasters, infinitely greater than those which had brought him to power.

They began with the invasion of the Low Countries by Germany's Army Group B under General von Bock, supported by Luftflotte 2 under General Kesselring. The northern Allied armies wheeled into Belgium to meet the assault, but despite the huge numbers of enemy warplanes striking deep into France, their advance was strangely unopposed from the air.

In fact the Allies were doing exactly what their enemies wanted. No sooner were they fully committed in Belgium than the tanks of General von Rundstedt's Army Group A, under cover of intense bombing by General Sperrle's Luftflotte 3, burst over the Meuse River at Sedan, to race northwards towards the Channel coast behind them. How successful the move was may be seen from the fact that all four German commanders just mentioned would shortly become field marshals.

For the Hurricane pilots in France the days became a nightmare of ceaseless activity as they battled against odds varying from heavy to impossible. On 11 May for instance, five of No. 1 Squadron's pilots, Flight Lieutenant Walker, Flying Officers Brown, Kilmartin and Richey and Sergeant Soper, sighted thirty Dornier Do 17s escorted by fifteen Messerschmitt Bf 110s near Sedan. The odds were thus exactly nine to one against – but they attacked immediately. Much to their delight the Dorniers retired to Germany but the 110s, which at this stage of the war were manned by crack crews, took up the challenge, still with a three to one advantage. Paul Richey in *Fighter Pilot* tells us what happened next:

We went in fast in a tight bunch, each picking a 110 and manoeuvring to get on his tail. I selected the rear one of two in line-astern who were turning tightly to the left. He broke away from his No 1 when he had done a half-circle and steepened his turn, but I easily turned inside him, holding my fire until I was within fifty yards and then firing a shortish burst at three-quarters deflection. To my surprise a mass of bits flew off him – pieces of engine-cowling and lumps of his glasshouse (hood) – and as I passed just over the top of him, still in a left-hand turn, I watched with a kind of fascinated horror as he went into a spin, smoke pouring out of him. I remember saying 'My God, how ghastly!' as his tail suddenly swivelled sideways and tore off, while flames streamed over the fuselage. Then I saw a little white parachute open beside it. Good!

Scarcely half a minute had passed, yet as I looked quickly around me I saw four more 110s go down – one with its tail off, a second in a spin, a third vertically in flames, and a fourth going up at forty-five degrees in a left-hand stall-turn with a little Hurricane on its tail firing into its side, from which burst a series of flashes and long shooting red flames. I shall never forget it.

All the 110s at my level were hotly engaged, so I searched above. 'Yes – those buggers up there will be a nuisance soon!' Three cunning chaps were out of the fight, climbing like mad in line-astern to get above us to pounce. I had plenty of ammunition left, so I climbed after them with the boost-override pulled. They were in a slight right-hand turn, and as I climbed I looked around. There were three others over on the right coming towards me, but they were below. I reached the rear 110 of the three above me. He caught fire after a couple of bursts and dived in flames. Then I dived at the trinity coming up from the right and fired a quick burst at the leader head-on.

I turned but they were still there; so were the other two from above. In a moment I was in the centre of what seemed a stack of 110s, although there were in fact only five . . . Although I was more manoeuvrable at this height than the Huns I found it impossible to get in an astern shot because every time I almost got one lined up tracers came whipping past from another on my tail . . .

After what seemed an age . . . I was flying down head-on at a 110 which was climbing up to me. We both fired – and I thought I had left it too late and we would collide. I pushed the stick forward violently. There was a stunning explosion right in front of me. For an instant my mind went blank. My aircraft seemed to be falling, limp on the controls. Then, as black smoke poured out of the nose and enveloped the hood, and a hot blast and a flicker of reflected flame crept into the dark cockpit, I said 'Come on – out you go!' [and baled out successfully] . . .

The entire population of [the village of] Rumigny had witnessed the fight and had seen six Huns come down nearby; they later found four more, making a total of ten. They watched me fighting the remaining five and said it had lasted at least fifteen minutes, perhaps more.

When I got back to the Squadron I found that Johnny [Walker] claimed to have shot down one definitely, and perhaps two, Hilly [Brown] two, Killy [Kilmartin] two and Soper two. With my two that made exactly the number found – ten – leaving the number I had fought as five (total fifteen as counted before the fight). The villagers on the ground had seen two enemy tails come off – presumably one was mine; the other was Killy's. The police presented me with one of the fins; with the black-and-white swastika pierced by two bullets, it made a respectable match for the First War fins we had with the Black Cross emblem on them.

After the war, German official records would give a rather different account, stating that only two Bf 110s had been lost. This therefore might be a good moment at which to deal with the vexed question of enemy casualties.

There is no doubt that on days of intense activity the RAF pilots did grossly overestimate the destruction they had inflicted. Such errors, inevitable with the sheer speed of air-fighting, were particularly exaggerated when large numbers of British fighters were involved, for as many as four pilots might hit the same enemy aircraft, each afterwards swearing that he had made a kill – in perfect good faith; on quieter days RAF claims were often less than the true enemy losses. This, however, in no way alters the fact that the post-war official figures cannot be relied upon either.

For a start the British post-war analysts misinterpreted the enemy records. For instance the Germans divided their losses between those incurred on 'war flights', on 'war support flights' and on non-combat flights. The assessors rightly omitted the last class but quite wrongly also omitted aircraft shot down on 'war support flights' such as air-sea rescue duties, which, as their very name implies, formed an essential part of the enemy's operations.

Furthermore the Luftwaffe stated its losses on a percentage basis. An aeroplane going down over enemy territory or in the sea was a 100 per cent loss but one which crashed behind its own lines was given a lesser percentage rating depending on what parts could be salvaged. This was appreciated to some extent and the British assessors included as destroyed those enemy aircraft treated as 80 per cent losses but the true total of machines destroyed was even higher for it should have included those rated by the Germans as low as a 60 per cent loss.

Above and beyond all this, however, the German records are clearly incomplete. This has been denied on the ground that the figures come from the Luftwaffe Quartermaster General's returns which were used as a basis for getting replacements. No commander in such a case, it is argued, would understate his losses. Yet the fact remains that there is no mention in these returns of German – and for that matter Italian – aircraft which were destroyed beyond doubt, wreckage and bodies being discovered and/or prisoners being taken. These incidents occurred not only in the Battle of France and the Battle of Britain but in North Africa, East Africa, the Balkans and Malta. Several reasons have been suggested for these discrepancies: that some of the Quartermaster General's returns have been lost; that the machines in question were older types which would not be replaced as such because their units were in the process of re-equipping with later versions; that there were alternative channels by which losses could be made good – a theory supported by the discovery that those units which are known to have suffered unreported losses did so on more than one occasion. But whatever the answer, that there are omissions from the official records remains unarguable.

Reverting to No. 1 Squadron's combat on 11 May, the pilots were all highly experienced; Richey's eyewitness account shows that he saw five enemy aircraft, including his own first victim, going down at one time, and he also shot down another 110 in flames later; the French confirmed the losses claimed on the ground; and all agreed there had been fifteen 110s at the start of the fight but only five engaging the luckless Richey – his colleagues having left the scene, out of ammunition – at the end of it. In these circumstances 1 Squadron's claims deserve far greater credence than any post-war assessment.

No. 1 Squadron was not of course the only Hurricane squadron in action. In the Air Component 85 and 87 Squadrons had been reinforced by 607 and 615 which had just converted from Gladiators, and on 10 May, 3 and 79 Squadrons flew out from Britain, as did No. 504 shortly afterwards. In the Advanced Air Striking Force, 1 and 73 Squadrons were joined on 10 May by 501 Squadron, among its pilots being Sergeant James Lacey, who now no longer flew with his undercarriage lowered. On 13 May he earned a Croix de Guerre by destroying a Bf 109, a Heinkel He 111 and a Bf 110, all confirmed by the French on the ground – all before breakfast. He was then attacked by four more 110s but escaped by some violent manoeuvres.

Also on 13 May, thirty-two more Hurricanes were flown out as

28

additional reinforcements, to be followed a little later by eight flights from different Hurricane units which were attached to squadrons already in France. These machines in total were the equivalent of six squadrons and their departure horrified Air Chief Marshal Sir Hugh Dowding, Commander-in-Chief of Fighter Command, who saw his precious Hurricanes wasting away before his eyes. His protests were so firm that no more Hurricanes were sent permanently across the Channel, though in order to bring them into action without too great a risk, other squadrons were ordered to France for the day, flying home by evening.

Among the squadrons thus engaged was No. 32 from Biggin Hill. Its first such mission is recorded in the Squadron Diary in the facetious style traditionally cultivated by the RAF, though later mocked by those who fail to realize that such an attitude helps to keep men sane:

> Whew! What a shock. Whole outfit up at 3:15 am. Going to France. Everyone amazed . . . Later all set off to France, land at Abbeville, refuel, hear dreadful stories, get very frightened, do a patrol, see nothing, feel better, do another, see nothing, feel much better, return to Biggin Hill, feel grand.

The cream of the joke was that the irrepressible diarist was Flight Lieutenant Michael Crossley, not only the finest pilot in the squadron but one of those rare, fortunate beings who never appear very frightened of anything.

On 19 May 32 Squadron found the war much more serious. Over Cambrai its pilots sighted a Dornier Do 17 with a strong escort of Bf 109s and Bf 110s. This suggested that the bomber either carried important personnel or was on an important recce mission. The Hurricanes attacked, losing one of their number whose pilot became a prisoner of war, but destroying the Dornier and perhaps as many as six of the escorting fighters. Three days later the squadron claimed another six 109s, this time without loss.

During the Battle of France the Luftwaffe by its own admission lost 1,284 aircraft in combat, plus nearly 200 more in accidents – and as we have seen its records are not complete. In the last ten days of May alone 129 officers and nearly 600 other ranks died, though some 400 prisoners were freed after the fall of France to fight again, if perhaps with somewhat diminished fervour. That Hurricanes must have been responsible for the majority of these losses is certain, if only because the Germans had encountered far more of them than any other Allied fighter.

They achieved this, moreover, despite operating under all possible disadvantages. Happily one of these at least was soon to be remedied. At this time many squadrons were still flying in the inflexible 'Vic' or 'Vee' formations where more time was spent in keeping station than in looking for hostile aircraft, and were still using standard copybook attacks, quite unsuited to high-speed combat, which the experienced Hurricane units had already rejected. Roland Beamont vividly describes what happened when 87 Squadron was joined by two less knowledge-able squadrons:

We made a fine sight as 36 Hurricanes formed up in the late afternoon sun in three squadron boxes, line-astern, four sections of Vic-threes to a squadron. I was flying No. 2 in the right-hand section of 87 Squadron, leading the Wing, and it made me feel quite brave looking back at so many friendly fighters. And then without fuss or drama about 10 Messerschmitt 109s appeared above the left rear flank of our formation out of some high cloud. The Wing leader turned in towards them as fast as a big formation could be wheeled, but the 109s abandoned close drill and, pulling their turn tight, dived one after the other on to the tail sections of the Wing. Their guns streamed smoke and one by one four Hurricanes fell away. None of us fired a shot – some never even saw it happen – and the enemy disengaged, while we continued to give a massive impression of combat strength over the battle area with four less Hurricanes than when we started. We had had more than three times the strength of the enemy on this occasion and had been soundly beaten tacti-cally by a much smaller unit, led with flexibility and resolution.

The Battle of France was soon over but the authorities were slow to react to facts and change the rules, and change came about the hard way by squadrons learning from experience and adapting themselves. Nevertheless, there were still some squadrons going into action in the beginning of the Battle of Britain in 'standard Fighter Command attacks', and many in the inflexible three-sections Vic formation. In 87 Squadron we had modified our tactics to an initial turn in towards the enemy when sighted, followed by flexible exploitation of the subsequent situation – in other words, every man for himself.[1]

Another disadvantage was that the dominant Luftwaffe was able to destroy Hurricanes on their own airfields, and indeed to put those airfields out of action. An eyewitness to one such attack was Charles Sims who was serving with the RAF at Vitry-en-Artois, the base for the Hurricanes of 607 Squadron. He recalls it in *The Royal Air Force: The First Fifty Years*:

Mid-morning on one of these days [in May 1940] saw No. 607 dispersed about its base, rearming and refuelling after a series of sorties against the enemy. Either by intelligent anticipation or listening in to the R/T wavelength of the Hurricanes, this moment was chosen by the Luftwaffe to attack them. The Me 109s and 110s came in low with their guns firing, determined to end once and for all this menace to their progress towards victory. They were, perhaps, a minute or two out in their reckoning, for whilst some Hurricanes were destroyed where they stood and some as they started up and took off, enough of them became airborne to bring about what must have been one of the most vicious low-level dog-fights in the war up to that time. The air above the airfield became a stage for twirling, turning and diving fighters, much too quick for the eye to follow, as aircraft dived into the ground or climbed away to chase each other, parachutes of victims opened or partly opened or caught fire whilst the noise of continuous machine-gun and cannon fire drowned the sound of bombing that was still going on farther afield. When it was all over – possibly in five minutes that seemed like an hour – and only smoke rose from the airfield, it was indeed a sorry sight to see.

Such was the resilience of the Hurricane and its pilots that that same afternoon 607 Squadron's remaining fighters, which had retired for a time to another airfield, effectively broke up a bomber formation attempting to repeat the morning raid. Clearly though, assaults like this could not be survived indefinitely, and as the German forces scythed across France they steadily overran the Hurricane bases. The constant moves to often quite inadequate landing grounds added to the physical pressures on the pilots. Sergeant Allard, 85 Squadron's leading 'ace', actually fell asleep in the cockpit as his Hurricane rolled to a standstill after his fifth flight of the day.

On top of this was the emotional strain. Having returned to his squadron following the action against the Bf 110s recounted earlier, Paul Richey found that:

> I had a hell of a headache and was jumpy and snappy. Often I dared not speak for fear of bursting into tears. I thought the explosion (probably a cannon shell in the front petrol tank) had concussed me slightly . . . I finally saw Doc Brown. He immediately ordered me off to bed for twenty-four hours and . . . gave me a couple of pills. After some time I slept.
>
> Scarcely had I dropped off when I was in my Hurricane rushing head-on at a 110. Just as we were about to collide I woke up with a jerk that nearly threw me out of bed. I was in a cold sweat, my heart banging wildly. I dropped off again – but the nightmare returned. This went on at intervals of about ten minutes all night. I shall never forget how I clung to the bed-rail in a dead funk. If there is ever a choice between physical and mental pain, I'll take physical every time.

It was no doubt this combination of bodily and mental exhaustion that indirectly brought about the death of 'Cobber' Kain, who by the end of the Battle of France had been credited with the destruction of seventeen enemy aircraft, making him one of the RAF's then top-scoring pilots. He was killed while 'beating up' his squadron's airfield prior to what would have been his return flight to Britain.

By 20 May exhaustion had reached such a level that few of the squadrons in France could have continued much longer, even had their remaining bases not been threatened by the panzers. The three Hurricane units in the Advanced Air Striking Force retired south, then west, ultimately to cover evacuations from Cherbourg and the Brest peninsula, in which tasks they were joined by the Hurricanes of 17 and 242 Squadrons, while the Air Component squadrons retired to Britain. Seventy-five of their Hurricanes had been lost to enemy action, a large proportion on the ground. No less than 120 more, damaged but repairable, had had to be burnt on the abandoned French airfields. Even the flight home was not without its perils, as exemplified by this report by Flying Officer Derek Ward, a member of 151 (Hurricane) Squadron who had only just flown out to join No. 87:

After being evacuated from Lille to Merville on Sunday evening, owing to the advance of the enemy, I landed at Merville at 1600 hours on Monday, 20 May. I was ordered to fly an unserviceable Hurricane home to Debden. This machine had no gunsight and all the instruments, except the compass, oil temp and pressure gauges, were U/S. The engine was badly over-heating and the oil temperature at minus one boost was 98°C. Seven guns were loaded but there was no incendiary or tracer to help with my aim.

I intended to land at Abbeville to collect some kit which I had left there on the way out. On approaching Abbeville I saw that the town was in flames and three Dornier 215s were dive-bombing the town. I climbed and attacked one of the three enemy aircraft and got in three bursts at 300 yards, without a gunsight, pointing my machine in the general direction of the aircraft. The Dornier dived into cloud. I followed and gave the enemy some more bursts in the cloud. I came out of cloud, circled for 10 minutes and saw another Do 215 between clouds and attacked again. My engine began to over-heat badly and 109s attacked me from behind. I dived into cloud and eventually landed at Abbeville.

I found that the Hurricane had a puncture in the starboard tank and the petrol was spraying out. The aerodrome was being evacuated and the U/S machines were being burned, chiefly Lysanders. The aerodrome crews were about to evacuate and they wished to burn my Hurricane rather than take the risk of starting it again owing to the petrol spraying out of the starboard tank. I stuck a bayonet several times into the starboard tank to empty it and managed to persuade two airmen to fill my port tank. I had to leave without the star-board tank being repaired and with only 50 rounds in each of the seven guns. I took off from Abbeville and two miles east of the aerodrome I encountered six Do 17s and six Me 109s. I attacked the leader of the 109s, which were coming head-on towards me, and I gave the leader a burst. He swerved left and I dived past him towards the ground. Fortunately the 109s continued on, escorting the bombers, and did not give chase. I flew my Hurricane over the Channel and landed at North Weald, England.[2]

Next day the Germans reached the Channel near Abbeville, trapping the northern Allied armies including the British Expeditionary Force. The surviving troops, covered by mainly French rearguards, retired to Dunkirk. Luckily the surrounding area, being criss-crossed with canals, was unsuitable for tank warfare and Hitler, already concerned at the number of his panzers that had been put out of action, was reluctant to risk further losses in such conditions – as indeed was his tank expert, General Guderian. Moreover it seemed to the Führer that there was no need to take the risk: Göring had assured him 'unconditionally' that the Luftwaffe could prevent the escape of a single soldier by sea.

That Göring's boast proved vain was caused in part by bad weather and in part by bad tactics. The Luftwaffe should have concentrated its assaults against the rescuing vessels rather than the men on the beaches; when it finally did so on 1 June, the evacuation was only able to continue by night. But the main reason why the German airmen failed to attain their objective was that they had to face the pilots of Fighter Command.

The RAF was not popular during or immediately following Dunkirk. Operating away from its bases, it could provide con-tinuous cover only by standing patrols, some of which inevitably encountered no enemy at all while others were swamped by over-whelming numbers. Many interceptions occurred out of sight of the beaches and the soldiers and sailors, understandably if unfairly, tended to assume that every aeroplane sighted was hostile. One treasures the experience of Flight Lieutenant Sir Archibald Hope of 601 Squadron, who was making his way home via Dunkirk after being shot down, when he had occasion to inform a high-ranking army officer that the aircraft the soldiers were reviling were in fact Hurricanes. The officer refused to believe him, protesting indignantly: 'But we've seen lots of those.'

Lots of Hurricanes might well have been seen, for during the evacuation from Dunkirk every available Hurricane squadron went into action. Their pilots were well aware of the feeling against them but they understood it, as is demonstrated by a letter home from one of their number, Flight Lieutenant Wight of 213 Squadron, which appears in the RAF Official History:[3]

Well, another day [28 May] is gone, and with it a lot of grand blokes. Got another brace of 109s today, but the whole Luftwaffe seems to leap on us – we were hopelessly out-numbered. I was caught napping by a 109 in the middle of a dog fight, and got a couple of holes in the aircraft, one of them filled the office with smoke, but the Jerry overshot and *he's* dead. If anyone says anything to you in the future about the inefficiency of the RAF – I believe the BEF troops were booing the RAF in Dover the other day – tell them from me we only wish we could do more. But without aircraft we can do no more than we have done – that is, our best, and that's fifty times better than the German best, though they are fighting under the most advantageous conditions. I know of no RAF pilot who has refused combat yet – and that sometimes means combat with odds of more than fifty to one. Three of us the other day had been having a fight, and were practically out of ammunition and juice when we saw more than eighty 109s with twelve Ju 87s, all the same we gave them combat, so much so that they left us alone in the end – on their side of the Channel too. This is not a tale of stirring heroism. It is just the work that we all do. One of my sergeants [Sergeant

Butterfield] shot down three fighters and a bomber [two Bf 109s, a Bf 110 and a Junkers Ju 88] before they got him – and then he got back in a paddle steamer. So don't worry, we are going to win this war . . . The spirit of the average pilot has to be seen to be believed.[4]

Nor did the completion of the Dunkirk operation mark the end of the Hurricane's fight in France. Apart from those in the Advanced Air Striking Force whose later exploits have already been mentioned, home-based Hurricane squadrons covered lesser evacuations or escorted Blenheims on bombing or reconnaissance missions up to the time of the French surrender. It was on one such raid on 7 June that Flight Lieutenant – later Group Captain – John Simpson won a DFC for an action later described in *Combat Report* by Hector Bolitho:

I singled out a Messerschmitt 109 and had a very exciting combat with him. He was a good pilot and he hit me several times. We began to do aerobatics and while he was on his back, I got in a burst which set him on fire. He jumped out, but I did not see his parachute open. His machine was almost burned out before it hit the ground. There were scores of fighters about me, but I still had plenty of ammunition. I got on the tail of another 109 and while I was firing at him two Messerschmitt 110s fired at me from either side. I continued to fire at the 109 which was badly winged. He suddenly stall-turned sharply to the right, went into a spin and crashed straight into one of the other Messerschmitts which was firing at me.

I couldn't resist following them down. It was a wonderful sight. They stuck together in a sort of embrace of flames, until they were a few hundred feet above the ground. Then they parted and crashed, less than 20 yards apart.

Few engagements at this time were so successful. In all 477 British fighters were lost in the Battle of France, the great majority of them, Hurricanes. One-fifth of the professional peacetime pilots were already dead or disabled, while about half their replacements were still totally inexperienced. And already German planners were turning their attention to an operation soon to be given the code name SEALION – the proposed invasion of Britain.

After the war was safely over, suggestions would be made that Hitler did not really intend to invade; it was all some monstrous bluff. Certainly Hitler would have preferred to have avoided a costly campaign if he could have persuaded the British to accept his terms. Had SEALION really been a bluff, however, the Germans would never have wasted time on innumerable conferences, involving almost all their senior staff officers, to thrash out details not only of the invasion but of the treatment of the conquered country thereafter. They would never have prepared a deception plan – a feint by escorted but empty merchant vessels into the North Sea. They would never have amended their plans from time to time, abandoning a suggested assault on Lyme Bay for instance – there is no point in amending a bluff. They would never have assembled so many barges, motor vessels and tugs in the Channel ports that they disrupted Germany's vitally important inland waterway transport. Above all they would never have risked crippling casualties to their Luftwaffe in daylight raids when it could have delivered night attacks which would have inflicted heavy damage with little possibility of being intercepted.

That the Luftwaffe did not do so was because night attacks could never achieve the elimination of Fighter Command – and that this was the preliminary requisite for an invasion was quite clear to both sides. Hitler first raised the possibility of invading on 2 July, though only 'provided that air superiority can be attained'. The Luftwaffe then began preliminary operations against British shipping in the Channel and by 16 July Hitler's intentions had become crystallized in his War Directive No 16:

> As England in spite of her hopeless military position still shows no sign of willingness to come to terms, I have decided to prepare, and if necessary to carry out a landing operation against her . . .
>
> The landing operation must be a surprise crossing on a broad front extending approximately from Ramsgate to a point west of the Isle of Wight . . .

The following preparations must be undertaken to make a landing in England possible:

The English air force must be eliminated to such an extent that it will be incapable of putting up any substantial opposition to the invading troops.

The British Chiefs of Staff had already reached a similar though more detailed conclusion. On 27 May they had reported to Churchill:

While our Air Force is in being, our Navy and Air Force together should be able to prevent Germany carrying out a serious sea-borne invasion of this country.

Supposing Germany gained complete air superiority, we consider that the Navy could hold up an invasion for a time, but not for an indefinite period.

If with our Navy unable to prevent it, and our Air Force gone, Germany attempted an invasion, our coast and beach defences could not prevent German tanks and infantry getting a firm footing on our shores. In the circumstances envisaged above our land forces would be insufficient to deal with a serious invasion.

The crux of the matter is air superiority.

If the invasion was to be thwarted therefore, everything depended on Britain's young fighter pilots. And on the pilots of one type of fighter in particular.

NOTES

1 Quoted in *Hurricane at War* by Chaz Bowyer.
2 Quoted in *Hurricane Squadron* by Perry Adams. Ward later rose to the rank of Squadron Leader, commanding 73 (Hurricane) Squadron in North Africa. He was killed in action on 17 June 1942.
3 *Royal Air Force 1939-1945* by Denis Richards and Hilary St G. Saunders – Volume I: *The Fight at Odds*.
4 Both Flight Lieutenant Wight – who was credited with destroying a total of six 109s over Dunkirk – and Sergeant Butterfield died fighting on 11 August 1940 during the Battle of Britain.

Chapter 4

Finest Hour

Twenty years later books and magazine articles began to appear decrying the merits of the Hurricane in the Battle of Britain, suggesting that it was inferior, outmoded and of such low performance as to somehow have contributed to the hazards of the time. How different were the true facts, for the Hurricane not only bore the brunt of the fighting but was exceptionally well fitted to do so.

The Hurricane, which was the first of the monoplane fighters to enter the Service, resulted from a brilliant design by Hawkers under Sydney Camm in 1934, and when it arrived in 111 Squadron in 1938 it was the fastest fighter of all at about 330 mph at its maximum power altitude.

By the outbreak of war in 1939 the Hurricane had been overtaken in this sense by the Spitfire and Me 109 with maximum speeds of about 350 mph, but to imply that a speed differential of 20 mph constituted operational inferiority would be to completely misunderstand the circumstances.

The Hurricane had an altogether exceptional combination of manoeuvrability, rugged strength, stability, ease of control and gun aiming, and viceless landing characteristics, which went far towards offsetting the fact that its climb, level and altitude performance were slightly lower than the Spitfire and Me 109. Hurricane pilots knew that once in combat they could outmanoeuvre any enemy and that with their eight

Browning machine-guns and the aiming accuracy of their aircraft, hitting the target was no problem.

Furthermore they knew that if in a tight spot the Hurricane could be pushed into a violent full power corkscrew dive which no Me 109 could follow; and that it could do this without serious consequences which was more than could be said for the 109 or the Spitfire, both of which developed unhealthy reputations for structural failure in high-speed dives . . .

In the cold figure of statistics it can be seen that the Hurricanes bore the brunt of the fighting in the battle [of Britain], but more than that . . . in late September 1940 with the battle at its height, there was a rumour to the effect that 87 [Squadron] were to be re-equipped with Spitfires, and there was such concern over this that the pilots asked the C.O. to intervene and prevent such a happening.

While this was going on Michael Lister Robinson, an old friend and C.O. of 609 at Warmwell and an acknowledged virtuoso of the Spitfire, came to see us in a new Spitfire 2. It was a beautiful aeroplane and much admired, and when he left, [Flight Lieutenant] Ian Gleed and I took off in our Hurricanes to escort him. Michael decided that the opportunity to have a go at us was too good to miss, but within one and a half turns we were firmly on his tail and after five or six exhilarating minutes at all levels and altitudes around Charmy Down, Michael gave it up and straightened out for Warmwell with a Hurricane firmly stationed on each side at two or three feet from his tailplane for a short time until with his superior speed he began to draw away.

If the Hurricane was an inferior fighter in the Battle of Britain, nobody told the pilots.

Such at least was the opinion of one of the Hurricane pilots, Roland Beamont in *Phoenix into Ashes*.[1] That the Hurricane bore the brunt of the Battle of Britain is beyond dispute. Hurricanes were responsible for 80 per cent of the interceptions of enemy aircraft during the battle and shot down more of them than all other fighters and all forms of ground defence put together. Nor was this surprising for Camm's insistence on his Hurricane's ease of production was now bearing golden fruit.

When the battle officially started on 10 July 1940, Dowding had available some 700 fighters, of which well over half were Hurricanes. There were two squadrons of two-seater Defiants which proved a failure in daylight operations, seven of converted Blenheims (including one operating solely at night), nineteen of Spitfires, and no less than twenty-seven of Hurricanes – Nos 1, 3, 17, 32, 43, 46, 56, 73, 79, 85, 87, 111, 145, 151, 213, 229, 238, 242, 249, 253, 257, 501, 504, 601, 605, 607 and 615. In addition another Hurricane squadron, No. 245, was stationed in Northern Ireland, while No. 263, though mainly equipped with twin-engined Whirlwinds, had a Hurricane flight for airfield defence. In Fighter Command's vital No. 11 Group, which under the New Zealander Air Vice-Marshal Keith Park guarded the south-east of England, there were three squadrons of Blenheims, six of Spitfires, fifteen of Hurricanes.

Moreover the speed with which Hurricanes were being produced – over 300 left the factories in June and about the same number in July – not only enabled these squadrons to make good the losses incurred in France, and not only ensured that throughout the battle the average strength of a Hurricane squadron was greater than that of any other fighter, but allowed a new Hurricane squadron, No. 232, to be formed on 16 July, and four more by the end of August.

Indeed at the very worst moments of the battle Dowding's main concern was not a shortage of Hurricanes but a shortage of Hurricane pilots. It is no coincidence that most of the pilots of the four Hurricane squadrons becoming operational during August came from other countries. No. 1 RCAF (later renumbered 401 to avoid confusion) obviously was manned by Canadians, Nos. 302 and 303 by Poles, and No. 310 by Czechs. Oddly enough though, the finest of all Czech pilots, Sergeant Josef Frantisek, who before his tragic death in a landing accident on 8 October had destroyed seventeen enemy aircraft including nine Bf 109s, flew with the Polish squadron, No. 303.

Of course, not even Hurricanes could be produced in sufficient quantities to match the numbers controlled by Göring, who on 19

July was promoted to the unique rank of Reichsmarschall with a special king-sized baton to prove it. He could muster 2,600 warplanes, not counting reconnaissance aircraft, in three *Luftflotten* (Air Fleets) stationed in France, the Low Countries, Denmark and Norway. Of these 50 per cent were serviceable at the beginning of July, 80 per cent by the end.

In the face of such odds it was fortunate indeed that Fighter Command enjoyed some compensating advantages. There was radar which gave warning of when and where the enemy would attack, though it was not very reliable in estimating the numbers of the attackers, notoriously unreliable in estimating their height and non-existent once they had crossed the coast when the defence relied solely on the eyes and ears of the gallant volunteers of the Observer Corps. Nor of course could radar report whether an attack was a genuine raid or a feint, a preliminary assault or the enemy's main effort. For this reason another vital card in the hands of the defenders was the high-frequency radio by which the controllers on the ground could give clear, direct instructions to the men in the sky, so enabling Fighter Command to achieve a degree of flexibility far beyond that of their foes.

Yet the defenders' greatest advantage was that of fighting over their own territory. A damaged British fighter which returned to base could be repaired to fight again, whereas a German warplane which was forced to land virtually undamaged was a 100 per cent loss to the Luftwaffe. A British airman who landed safely by parachute could be in action again within hours, while a German airman became a prisoner of war. And it was in just these areas that more of the Hurricane's virtues became so valuable.

It will have been noted already that the Hurricane repeatedly proved capable of surviving the most murderous punishment. Its simple design then enabled it to be repaired comparatively quickly, either by its squadron's ground crews or, in more serious cases, by a group of units called the Hurricane Repair Network, entrusted with this task. During the Battle of Britain 60 per cent of the Hurricanes which came down on land were able to return to service and indeed 35 per cent of the fighters issued to the squadrons were repaired aircraft. During the whole war more than 4,000 damaged Hurricanes were restored by the Repair Network, but even when the Hurricane became a total loss it frequently remained aloft at least until its still more valuable pilot could escape by parachute.

These factors became apparent from the earliest days of the battle. On 10 July the Hurricanes of 111 Squadron scattered a formation of Dornier Do 17s with a head-on attack, though at the cost of the life of Flying Officer Higgs who crashed into one of the bombers. The escorting 109s then intervened and Flying Officer Ferris, having downed one, was engaged by three more which shot away an aileron control – in spite of which he was able to land safely. In all eleven enemy aircraft were destroyed on this day, one by unknown means, one by AA guns, two by Spitfires, seven by Hurricanes. The only Hurricane lost was that of Higgs.

The pattern was repeated next day. Two Spitfires were lost together with their pilots, but of four Hurricanes which fell only one pilot died – even he baled out but was drowned. The Luftwaffe lost seventeen machines, one to causes unknown, two to Blenheims, fourteen to Hurricanes. One of the fourteen was a Dornier Do 17 shot down by Squadron Leader Douglas Bader who had been ordered to intercept an intruder reported off the east coast. He relives the experience in *Fight for the Sky*:

There was low cloud at about 600 feet and drizzle; the visibility seemed to be about two miles . . . I took off and discovered the cloud base was exactly 700 feet. I remember thinking what a splendid view the Hurricane had under such conditions.

At the coast the cloud base had lifted to 1,000 feet. I flew along towards Cromer wondering what on earth a German could be doing flying round the Norfolk coast below cloud.

Then I saw him 400 yards in front of me. As I closed on him I recognized the narrow fuselage and twin fins of a Dornier 17, the aeroplane nicknamed the 'flying pencil'. The enemy had not seen me. I imagine the crew did not expect to be intercepted at that height in that weather and were taking it a bit easy. Anyhow we continued flying along with my Hurricane gaining on the Dornier. At 250 yards, I had just re-set my reflector sight to 200 yards range when the enemy

43

rear-gunner opened fire. The flashes from his machine-gun were vivid. That crew had woken up! . . .

I remember thinking to myself as the Dornier gunner opened fire on me: 'I've got a twelve-cylinder engine shielding me, a bullet-proof windscreen *and* eight machine-guns.' I was totally relaxed. I fired at the Dornier, observing no effect other than a steeply banked turn to the left, but he was still below the cloud. I followed him round and he straightened up after a complete 180 degrees. Then he started a shallow climb into cloud, with me in position behind him. I fired a second burst as he disappeared and continued into cloud behind him, still shooting. With blistering curses I gave him up and flew back to Coltishall where I reported failure to the Operations Room.

About fifteen minutes later the Controller telephoned to say that a Home Guard observation post had reported a Dornier crashing into the sea near Cromer at the exact time of my action.[2] This proved a lucky start for the new C.O. of 242 Squadron. After the incident, I remember thinking how easy it had been shooting from the Hurricane. Apart from the smell of cordite in the cockpit and the noise of the guns I might have been keeping line-astern formation on the Dornier at some peace-time air display.

Nonetheless Göring was in an optimistic mood as July came to an end. The Luftwaffe had already achieved one essential preliminary to the invasion by sinking four destroyers, thereby forcing the Royal Navy to abandon Dover as a base. In addition it had greatly overestimated the casualties it had inflicted on Fighter Command. Accordingly Göring issued orders for a major offensive. It was to commence on 10 August which would be code-named ADLERTAG – 'Eagle Day'. He considered that four days would see the destruction of all fighter airfields south of a line between Chelmsford and Gloucester. A further four weeks would complete the elimination of Britain's defences – just right for the launching of SEALION in mid-September.

As a kind of dress rehearsal, major attacks of unprecedented intensity were flung against convoys in the Channel on 8 August.

They cost the Luftwaffe twenty-seven aircraft. The fate of one is unknown; four fell to Spitfires which lost three of their own number together with their pilots; all the other twenty-two were destroyed by Hurricanes, though eleven of these were also lost, as were nine of their pilots. The Hurricanes of 145 Squadron had a particularly dramatic day. In the early morning they broke up a large raid, destroying three Messerschmitt Bf 109s and two Junkers Ju 87 Stuka dive-bombers at the cost of two pilots killed. At midday they shot down two further Stukas without loss. Finally in the late afternoon three more of their pilots died but enemy records confirm their destruction of one 109, two 110s and five Stukas. This was not the way for the Luftwaffe to achieve air supremacy.

Bad weather forced a postponement of Eagle Day but, following heavy preliminary strikes on the 11th and 12th, this finally took place on 13 August – only for the weather to disrupt Göring's plans again. The Messerschmitt Bf 110s which were detailed to protect Dornier Do 17s making for the Thames Estuary were recalled because of the weather but the bombers did not receive the order so bravely pushed on alone. One section was intercepted by the Hurricanes of 111 and 151 Squadrons which between them shot down five Dorniers, and although another section bombed the aerodrome at Eastchurch, this was not a Fighter Command but a Coastal Command base. To balance this error, a group of Bf 110s appeared over Portland minus the bombers they were supposed to be guarding – they stayed only long enough to lose one of their number to the guns of a Hurricane of 238 Squadron manned by Flying Officer Hughes.

During the day the Luftwaffe lost in all forty-five aircraft to fighters, AA guns or accident, the Hurricanes' share being at least twenty-five. On the other hand twelve of the thirteen RAF machines destroyed were Hurricanes, although only three of their pilots were killed. Four more Hurricanes were badly damaged but returned safely.

The Luftwaffe made its greatest effort on 15 August. The first raids were as usual directed against airfields in the South-East. 501 Squadron broke up a strong raid of Stukas, shooting down two of them. Two Hurricanes also fell but, as so often, both pilots baled out. Pilot Officer Truran of 615 Squadron, attacked by 109s, had his Hurricane hit in the rear fuselage by cannon shells which caused a small fire, while its wings were riddled by machine-gun bullets – but again, as so often, he was able to land safely.

As the early raiders retired, a strong force of Heinkel He 111s escorted by Bf 110s from Norway struck across the North Sea. They lost fifteen of their number, nine of them to Hurricanes, among these being 605 Squadron which flew 80 miles from the Firth of Forth to take part in the action. The Hurricane of one member of this squadron, Pilot Officer Law, was heavily damaged but it still got him back over the coast before crash-landing. A follow-up raid by Junkers Ju 88s from Denmark was unlucky enough to encounter the Hurricanes of 73 Squadron which shot down seven of them without loss.

In the afternoon the attacks switched back to the South. The frantic nature of the fighting that followed is well illustrated by the Combat Report of 87 Squadron's Pilot Officer Trevor Jay:

> A Ju 87 crossed my sights, I fired and the pilot baled out. I attacked a second Ju 87 which blew up and caught fire. I was then attacked by Me 110s and dived into cloud to escape. I climbed up again and ran into five Me 109s which attacked me, I concentrated on one and he went down with black smoke coming out. I then finished my ammunition and was shot down by the other Me 109s.[3]

A final raid was directed against Croydon aerodrome by *Erprobungsgruppe* (Test Group) 210, a unit specializing in precision attacks. 111 Squadron, based at Croydon, was able to get airborne just in time and moments later the enemy aircraft were themselves attacked by the Hurricanes of 32 Squadron which shot down a Bf 110 and a Bf 109. They also gave 111 Squadron the opportunity to gain height and its Hurricanes now made a head-on assault which resulted in the destruction of five Bf 110s, including the one flown by the enemy commander, Hauptmann (Captain) Walter Rubensdörffer.

The death of their finest bomber pilot must have completed the Germans' misery. 'Black Thursday' had cost them seventy-five warplanes of which sixty-seven fell to RAF fighters. The Hurricanes' share was at least thirty-eight, possibly over fifty; there were of course many more Hurricanes involved. Equally, a majority of the RAF's losses – seventeen out of twenty-eight – were Hurricanes, though ten of their pilots survived.

Twenty more RAF aircraft were lost in combat on 16 August. Eleven of these were Hurricanes, seven of whose pilots were saved. Forty-three enemy aircraft fell to the guns of the defending fighters – forty-eight in all. The Hurricanes downed at least twenty, possibly twenty-five. A useful proportion of this total was gained by 43 Squadron which intercepted an unescorted formation of Stukas, of which it shot down seven. Two Hurricanes were shot down as well but both pilots were unharmed.

Yet the incident which in a sense symbolized the exploits of the Hurricane pilots was strictly an individual one. Flight Lieutenant James Brindley Nicolson of 249 Squadron, who had never previously fired his guns in anger, was about to attack a hostile formation when his Hurricane was struck from behind by four cannon shells. He later gave an account – repeated in Chaz Bowyer's *Hurricane at War* – of what followed:

The first shell tore through the hood over my cockpit and sent splinters into my left eye. One splinter, I discovered later, nearly severed my eyelid. I couldn't see through that eye for blood. The second cannon shell struck my spare petrol tank and set it on fire. The third shell crashed into the cockpit and tore off my right trouser leg. The fourth shell struck the back of my left shoe and made quite a mess of my left foot . . . I was just thinking of jumping out when suddenly a Messerschmitt 110 whizzed under me and got right in my gunsights . . . I pressed the gun button, for the Messerschmitt was in nice range; I plugged him the first time and I could see my tracer bullets entering the German machine . . .

By this time it was pretty hot inside my machine from the burst petrol tank. I couldn't see much flame, but I reckon it was there all right. I remember looking once at my left hand which was keeping the throttle open. It seemed to be in the fire itself and I could see the skin peeling off it. Yet I had little

47

pain. Unconsciously too, I had drawn my feet up under my parachute on the seat, to escape the heat I suppose. Well, I gave the German all I had, and the last I saw of him was when he was going down, with his right wing lower than the left wing. I gave him a parting burst and as he had disappeared, started thinking about saving myself. I decided it was about time I left the aircraft and baled out . . .

[When descending by parachute] an aircraft – a Messerschmitt I think – came tearing past me. I decided to pretend I was dead, and hung limply by the parachute straps. The Messerschmitt came back once, and I kept my eyes closed, but I didn't get the bullets I was half-expecting. I don't know if he fired at me; the main thing is that I wasn't hit.

While I was coming down like that, I had a good look at myself. I could see the bones of my left hand showing through the knuckles. Then for the first time I discovered I'd been wounded in the foot. Blood was oozing out of the lace holes of my left boot. My right hand was pretty badly burned too . . .

Finally I touched down in [a] field and fell over.[4] Fortunately it was a still day. My parachute just floated down and stayed down without dragging me along, as they some-times do. I had a piece of good news almost immediately. One of the people who came along and who had watched the combat, said they had seen the Messerschmitt 110 dive straight into the sea.

Nicolson recovered from his numerous injuries to record his experience – and to receive the only Victoria Cross ever awarded to a pilot of Fighter Command.

Ironically the events of 15 and 16 August, which the enemy had believed would exhaust Fighter Command, exhausted the Luftwaffe instead; so much so that although the 17th was a fine day, only a few reconnaissance aircraft crossed the coast. By the 18th though, the Germans were back in force. The Hurricanes suffered severely on this occasion, twenty-nine of the thirty-five RAF fighters which fell being Hurricanes. Only nine of their pilots died and eight of the Hurricanes lost even brought their pilots home, although they were so badly damaged that they had to be written off. In return 56 Squadron alone downed six Bf 110s without loss, while of the sixty-five German warplanes destroyed by fighters (ground defences or accidents claimed five more) at least thirty-two, possibly thirty-seven were the victims of Hurricanes.

Once more the enemy paused before resuming mass attacks. This was just as well for when these recommenced on 24 August, they finally began to strike at the heart of the defences. Although German Intelligence was abysmal throughout the battle, German pilots, by using their eyes and brains, had located the RAF's vital sector stations which exercised operational control of the squadrons in the air. If these could be knocked out, it would paralyze Fighter Command.

From 24 August to 6 September therefore the Luftwaffe mounted almost continuous attacks on the sector stations, heavily damaging Debden in Essex, Hornchurch and North Weald just north of London, Kenley and particularly Biggin Hill just south of the capital. As their control of their fighters became less effective, so casualties among these increased, for now they were frequently attacked as they climbed or even occasionally as they took off.

By now the Messerschmitt Bf 110 was being used mainly in the fighter-bomber role and in any event the Hurricane almost always proved its superior in combat. The Hawker fighters' most significant success at this time came on 4 September when 253 Squadron engaged a strong force of 110s attempting to bomb the Hawker works at Brooklands. They shot down six, all confirmed on the ground, and so shook the survivors that these bombed the Vickers factory making Wellington bombers by mistake – though very effectively, it must be admitted. Two days later the Luftwaffe tried again but on this occasion No. 1 Squadron intercepted, downed two 110s and prevented any real damage.

There was also no doubt that provided the Hurricane could gain altitude in time, it proved more than capable of dealing with the Luftwaffe's finest fighter. On 30 August, for instance, Squadron Leader Gleave, of 253 Squadron, personally claimed four Bf 109s, the destruction of which was later confirmed by enemy records. The most successful Hurricane squadron in encounters with 109s during this period was No. 85; on 28 August it gave a demonstration of its skill to Winston Churchill who was visiting the south-east coastal defences. The Squadron Diary tells the story:

Croydon, 28/8/40. Ten Hurricanes took off at 1602 hours to patrol Tenterden and were then ordered to intercept Raid 15. About 20 Me 109s were sighted at 1625 hours flying at 18,000 feet in the Dungeness area. One Me 110 was seen at the same time in the same vicinity.

The squadron approached from the sun, but were spotted at the last moment by E/A [Enemy Aircraft] who appeared not to be anxious to engage and broke formation in all directions. Six Me 109s were destroyed and 1 Me 110 damaged.

Sqn Ldr Townsend gave a two-three second burst and E/A rolled over and dived steeply, seen going down by Flt Lt Hamilton and Fg Off Gowers, both of whom saw black and white smoke coming out of E/A. Sqn Ldr Townsend estimated his position at about 12 miles NW of Lympne. This confirmed by Maidstone Observer Corps who received a report at 1646 that a Me 109 had crash-landed at R5167, the pilot being taken prisoner. Plt Off Allard attacked E/A at 200 yds, closing to 20 yards and it caught fire and dived vertically into the sea, two-three miles outside Folkestone harbour. Witnessed by Plt Off English. He then fired several short bursts at another Me 109 which was making for France. E/A dived and flew at 20 feet from sea but engine failed with black smoke coming out, position then was about 5 miles N of St Inglevert, which was confirmed by 11 Group signal 11G/174 of 29/8. Plt Off Hodgson chased E/A from 17,000 ft down across the Channel to 20 ft above sea level. Fired several bursts and saw pieces falling off and only 1/3 of rudder left. E/A was going very slowly when last seen and emitting much black smoke. Plt Off Hodgson had to turn back when 5 miles NW of Cap Gris Nez owing to lack of ammunition but he was certain E/A was finished. This was confirmed by 11 Group Signal 11G/174 of 29/8.

Fg Off Woods-Scawen attacked E/A from quarter

following to astern and gave two long bursts. Black smoke and what appeared to be petrol from the wing tanks poured out of E/A and it dived down vertically. He followed it down for several thousand feet and left it when it was obviously out of control. It was believed to have crashed near Dungeness and this was confirmed by Maidstone Observer Corps who reported a Me 109 in the sea Dymchurch at 1640.

Sgt Walker-Smith attacked Me 109 and the port petrol tank was seen to explode and then [E/A] went into steep dive. At that moment Sgt Walker-Smith was fired at and had to take evasive action but immediately afterwards dived and saw a large explosion on the sea and black smoke. Plt Off Hodgson confirmed having seen a Me 109 dive into the sea at this point. Fg Off Gowers attacked Me 110 from astern and saw bullets entering but it went into a shallow dive towards French coast and got away. Fg Off Gowers used all his ammunition and definitely damaged E/A.

The Me 109s all had yellow wing tips.

Enemy casualties: 6 Me 109s destroyed, 1 Me 110 damaged.

Our Casualties: Nil.

It will be noted that 85 Squadron did its utmost to verify its successes. That only four of the 109s claimed can be located in German records again suggests that one of the enemy units involved had channels other than the Quartermaster General's returns by which it could make good its losses.

In fact the Hurricane pilots' most dangerous foe by now was not the 109 but their own fatigue – as 85 Squadron's subsequent experiences show all too clearly. On 31 August the pilots were involved in three actions on the same afternoon. In the first they were bombed as they took off, then attacked from above. They claimed two 109s and a 110 but lost two Hurricanes. Pilot Officer Worrall baled out unhurt, but Squadron Leader Townsend was taken to hospital with a foot wound. In the second 85 Squadron destroyed three 109s and one Hurricane force-landed without injury to the pilot. The third is thus described in the Squadron Diary:

Nine Hurricanes took off Croydon 1917 hours to patrol Hawkinge and were then ordered to intercept Raid 18C. The first indication of position of E/A was given by AA fire from Dover and then nine Me 109 were seen flying at about 15,000 feet. The squadron circled out to sea as E/A passed on left, then wheeled in and caught them by surprise when individual combats ensued.

Plt Off Allard opened fire on E/A from 150 yards astern and parts of the wing appeared to break off. E/A dived down and crashed near Folkestone either on land or just in the sea.

Fg Off Woods-Scawen carried out beam attack causing E/A to dive steeply, then gave a further burst from astern and E/A went down on fire with wing tank burning – confirmed by Plt Off Lewis.

Plt Off Lewis fired a four-seconds burst at E/A from 150 yards on the beam and from slightly below. Black smoke billowed out and E/A dived steeply. Plt Off Lewis followed it down to 5,000 feet making sure it was done for and rejoined squadron. Position then above sea near Folkestone.

Fg Off Gowers fired two bursts of five seconds and seven seconds, caused a large piece to blow out of port wing of E/A. Petrol streamed out as E/A dived vertically and when Gowers left him at 4,000 feet he was still diving straight down and by then was in flames. Confirmed by Plt Off Lewis.

Nine Hurricanes landed Croydon 2005 hours to 2022 hours.

Enemy Casualties: 4 Me 109 destroyed.

Our losses: Nil.

All the four enemy fighters claimed were subsequently confirmed by German records.

On 1 September, however, the pressure finally told on 85 Squadron and four Hurricanes were lost in combat. Flying Officer Woods-Scawen's body was found nearly a week later, his parachute unopened; Sergeant Booth's parachute caught fire – he clung to life for six and a half months before dying; Sergeant Ellis was never seen again; Flying Officer Gowers did bale out safely but not without severe burns and wounds to hands and feet.

Next day another Hurricane pilot died when his parachute failed to open. Pilot Officer Anthony Woods-Scawen of 43 Squadron had survived his brother Patrick by less than twenty-four hours.

Yet despite such heartbreaking losses, which by 6 September had reduced Fighter Command to its lowest level of both machines and men, the defenders stuck tenaciously to their task. They would soon receive their reward, for already a chain of events was being forged which would lift the intolerable pressure from them.

On the night of 24–25 August a few German bombs had fallen, quite accidentally, in the centre of London. Next night Bomber Command retaliated with a raid on Berlin, which it repeated twice more before the end of the month. The damage done was minimal but the German public was stunned and an enraged Hitler gave permission for reprisals to be directed against the British capital.

This did not necessarily mean that these reprisals had to take place, but in fact Göring was all in favour of them. He believed that they would help to prepare the way for the invasion by shattering communications and perhaps compelling the British government to move elsewhere, and that they would also force Dowding to commit his final reserves of fighters which the Reichsmarschall considered were being held back deliberately. In the last resort though, it seems that the unspectacular hammering of the sector stations had little appeal for Göring; he much preferred a dramatic assault on London which would mask the exposure of his famous boast that no enemy warplane would ever violate German airspace.

Göring's assault was made on 7 September by nearly 350 bombers, escorted by over 600 fighters – and at first he believed he had achieved a significant success. The defenders, trying to guard against the anticipated strikes on airfields, failed to intercept the German armada which was thus able to inflict terrible damage on London's East End. Then when the British fighters belatedly intervened, they were overwhelmed by Bf 109s as they climbed – though once more the ruggedness of the Hurricane did at least reduce pilot casualties. One of the pilots concerned was Sub-Lieutenant – later Commander – 'Dickie' Cork, who along with other Fleet Air Arm officers had been 'loaned' to the RAF in its hour of need and was serving with 242 Squadron. In a letter home, set out by David Masters in *So Few*, he recalls what happened to him:

We ran into about 200–250 German bombers and fighters . . . Unfortunately or not, I don't know, I was flying in the first section with the C.O. [Bader] and before we knew where we were we found ourselves in the middle of all this mass. Every way you turned all you could see were German machines – and there was some lead flying about the sky! Anyway we stuck together and got out of it without injury except a few scratches from glass and odd bits of bullets, but you should have seen our machines – absolutely full of holes and they couldn't even make one whole aircraft out of what was left.[5]

Nonetheless, for all the defenders' misfortunes, the tide had in practice turned in their favour. With its bases no longer under direct attack, Fighter Command had a chance to rest exhausted pilots, even to mount training sorties for new arrivals. It also had more time in which to bring off favourable interceptions – during the next few days, raids on London were so hounded by fighters that many were dispersed before they could reach their objective.

Unfortunately on 14 September co-ordination of the interceptions broke down badly and the RAF suffered heavily in consequence. Hitler, who had started to have doubts, regained his optimism. He ordered all preparations for the invasion to continue, declared the achievements of the Luftwaffe 'above all praise', and instructed Göring to make one last great effort on 15 September – when excellent weather was forecast – and shatter the defences for ever.

Apart from reconnaissance or minor diversionary missions, the Luftwaffe's operations on 15 September consisted of two massive raids, one in the morning, one in the afternoon. The morning attack, made by about 100 Dornier Do 17s, escorted by over 300 fighters, took some time to assemble over the French coast and so gave Fighter Command plenty of warning. On its way to London the hostile formation was engaged by five Spitfire squadrons and the Hurricanes of 229, 253, 303 and 501 Squadrons, but it was still intact as it neared the capital. At this point Bader's 12 Group Wing attacked it from the flank, the two Spitfire squadrons engaging the 109s, the three Hurricane squadrons the Dorniers. Simultaneously four more Hurricane squadrons charged the bombers head-on.

The Hurricane squadrons in question might have been selected to typify Fighter Command: 242 Squadron as a mainly Canadian outfit represented what were then called the British Dominions; the Poles of 302 and the Czechs of 310 Squadrons represented the 'Free' Air Forces from the occupied countries; 17, 73 and 257 were regular Royal Air Force squadrons; 504, the County of Nottingham Squadron, symbolized the Auxiliary Air Force. And between them they routed the bomber formation, Bader later giving a typically forthright summary of the action:

Patrolled south of Thames (approximately Gravesend Area) at 25,000 feet. Saw two squadrons pass underneath us in formation travelling NW in purposeful manner. Then saw AA bursts, so turned Wing and saw enemy aircraft 3,000 feet below to the NW. Managed perfect approach with two other squadrons between our Hurricanes and sun and enemy aircraft below and down sun. Arrived over enemy aircraft formation of twenty to forty Do 17s: noticed Me 109 dive out of sun and warned our Spitfires to look out . . . Opened fire at 100 yards in steep dive and saw a large flash behind starboard motor of Dornier as wing caught fire: must have hit petrol pipe or tank . . . Finally ran out of ammunition chasing crippled and smoking Do 17 into cloud. It was the finest shambles I've been in, since for once we had position, height and numbers. Enemy aircraft were a dirty looking collection.[6]

It says much for the courage of the German aircrews that in the afternoon another attack was launched by three separate groups, totalling 150 Dornier Do 17s, Heinkel He 111s and Junkers Ju 88s, escorted once more by over 300 fighters. The Hurricanes of 213 and 607 Squadrons intercepted one formation, engaging it so fiercely that some of the bombers turned back. Most though did reach London where again they were scattered by a mass of defending fighters. Sub-Lieutenant Cork of 242 Squadron was once more in the thick of the action as his Combat Report demonstrates:

Whilst flying as Red 2 in the leading section of the squadron we sighted the enemy to the south and well above us. We climbed as fast as possible to the attack but on the way were attacked by a number of Me 109s. The order was given on R/T to break formation, so I broke sharply away with a Me on my tail. I was now in a dive and suddenly flew through the second squadron in the Wing formation and lost the enemy machine; at the same time I saw a Do 17 on my starboard, flying NW. I dived 6,000 feet to attack and fired a long burst at the port engine, which started to smoke. I attacked again on the beam – large pieces of enemy machine flew off and his starboard wing burst into flames near the wing tip. He dived straight into the cloud, heading towards a clear patch, so I waited till he came into the open and fired another burst in a head-on attack and the machine dived into the ground.

I climbed up 1,000 feet and was attacked by two yellow-nosed Me 109s from above, so I did a steep turn to left and managed to get on the tail of one, fired a very short burst, and then ran out of ammunition. No damage was seen on enemy machine, but as I was being attacked from behind by a second fighter I went into a vertical dive down to 2,000 feet and returned to base. No damage to my own machine.

Göring's great effort had cost him twenty Messerschmitt Bf 109s, three Messerschmitt Bf 110s, three Junkers Ju 88s, ten Heinkel He 111s and twenty-two Dornier Do 17s, plus a couple of flying-boats. Six aircraft were lost to accidents, one to AA fire, fifty-three to fighters. Spitfires made at least ten kills but probably less than twenty; Hurricanes – of which as usual there were many more involved – at least thirty but probably less than forty. Six Spitfires were lost, as were four of their pilots; twenty Hurricanes were shot down but only eight of their pilots died.

Two days later the lessons of 15 September were discussed at Hitler's Headquarters. Its War Diary bluntly records the conclusions reached:

> The enemy air force is still by no means defeated; on the contrary it shows increasing activity. The weather situation as a whole does not permit us to expect a period of calm. The Führer therefore decides to postpone SEALION indefinitely.

NOTES

1 This rather odd title derives from the fact that it is mainly an account of the decline of the British aircraft industry after the war.
2 Its loss was also confirmed by enemy records.
3 Jay in fact force-landed his Hurricane which was later repaired. He was killed on 24 October 1940 following a mid-air collision with a fellow member of his squadron. The other Hurricane returned safely with a good deal of its tail missing but the propeller of Jay's aircraft was shattered. He was forced to bale out and his parachute failed to open.
4 Nicolson tactfully omitted to mention that he was shot again just before he landed by a trigger-happy Local Defence Volunteer.
5 Understandably enough, Cork played down the extent of his injuries. In reality he had been hit in the face and eyes by splinters from a shattered windscreen. He was taken to hospital – protesting that he was 'fine' – but happily made a rapid recovery and rejoined his squadron within the week.
6 Quoted in *The Battle of Britain August–October 1940* an official – though it must be said, not very accurate – Air Ministry account.

Chapter 5

Cover of Darkness

Despite Hitler's decision and the subsequent dispersal of the barges and transports from the invasion ports, Göring at first persisted with his daylight attacks, though they grew steadily less effective and more pointless. Their main aim appears to have been to bolster the Reichsmarschall's crumbling prestige. Certainly they never looked like crippling Fighter Command. On the contrary, on 8 October yet another new Hurricane squadron, No. 312, with mainly Czech personnel, gained its first victory, shooting down a Junkers Ju 88 on a reconnaissance flight. This put up an admirable resistance, damaging no fewer than three Hurricanes, all of which nevertheless returned safely to base.

Indeed before 1940 ended, the Hurricane had become more than ever the RAF's most important fighter. Though the Hurricane flight of 263 Squadron had disappeared, No. 247. the last Gladiator unit in Britain, had finally converted to Hurricanes, while eight new Hurricane squadrons had been formed, including a second Canadian unit, two more of Poles and No. 71, the first Eagle Squadron of American volunteers. Five further squadrons, including three Polish ones, had received the Hawker fighters by the end of March 1941.

The futility of the enemy's daylight operations reached its height – or depth – on 11 November. On that day ten Fiat BR 20 bombers escorted by about forty Fiat CR 42 biplane fighters of the Italian Air Force, the Regia Aeronautica, attempted to attack shipping off Harwich. They met the Hurricanes of 46 and 257 Squadrons which shot down three bombers and three fighters without loss, and in future they made raids on Britain only at night.

The Luftwaffe had already turned to night attacks, directed principally against London but also at Britain's industrial cities. In the future the bombers would be opposed chiefly by twin-engined Beaufighters fitted with AI (Airborne Interception) radar sets, but the aircraft were slow coming into service and the operators took some time to get used to their new and temperamental equipment. During the winter of 1940–41 the Luftwaffe therefore found itself up against some more familiar opponents.

Hurricane pilots had engaged enemy raiders operating under cover of darkness during and even before the Battle of Britain. Back as far as the night of 26–27 June, Squadron Leader Max Aitken of 601 had earned a DFC for such a success. His account is repeated in *Fight for the Sky*[1] by Bruce Barrymore Halpenny:

At midnight the operational phone rang and I received orders to patrol a certain line. As I ran out to my fighter plane I could hear the sirens wailing in a neighbouring town. There was no moon and quite a lot of cloud. I took off and climbed through the clouds. I was excited, for I had waited for this chance for the previous three nights, sitting in a chair all night dressed in my flying clothes and yellow-painted rubber life jacket which we call 'Mae West'.

I climbed to the height ordered and remained on my control line. After about an hour, I was told by wireless that the enemy were at a certain spot flying from north-west to south-east.

Luckily, I was approaching that spot myself. The searchlights, which had been weaving about beneath light cloud, suddenly all converged at one spot.

They illuminated the cloud brilliantly, and there silhouetted on the cloud, flying across my starboard beam were three enemy aircraft. I turned to port and slowed down slightly. One searchlight struck through a small gap and showed up the whole of one plane. I recognized it as a Heinkel 111.

One of the enemy turned to port. I lost sight of the other.

I fastened on the last of the three. I got about 100 yd behind and below, where I could clearly see his exhaust flames. As we went out of the searchlights and crossed the coast he went into a shallow dive.

This upset me a bit, for I got rather high almost directly behind him, but I managed to get back and opened my hood to see better. I put my firing button to fire and pressed it. Bullets poured into him. It was at point blank range; I could see the tracer disappearing inside but nothing seemed to happen except that he slowed down considerably. I almost overshot him, but put the propeller into the full 'fine' pitch and managed to keep my position. I fired again in four bursts, and then noticed a glow inside the German machine. We had been in a shallow dive, and I thought we were getting near the sea; so I fired all the rest of my ammunition into him. The red glow got brighter. He was obviously on fire inside. At 500 ft I broke away to the right and tried to follow, but overshot so I did not see him strike the water.

I climbed and at 1,000 ft pulled off a parachute flare. As the flare fell towards the sea I saw the Heinkel lying on the water. A column of smoke was blowing from his rear section. I circled twice, but there was no movement, no one tried to climb out so I turned and flew for home.

Such sorties, however, had been one-off missions at times when Hurricanes could be spared from more urgent tasks. Now 73 Squadron, followed by 85, 87, 96 (one of the new squadrons formed in December) and 151 converted completely to night operations, while experienced pilots from most other Hurricane units were called upon to meet specific raids after dark as the need arose. Their duties were both dangerous and difficult as Squadron Leader 'Doug' Nicholls, at that time a sergeant with 151 Squadron, makes clear:

It was amazing how many people crashed on take off at night. They seemed to get to about four or five hundred feet and then were unable to adjust their eyes from visual control to instrument control, they just seemed to lose it and we had about four or five people just slide over, lose their direction altogether, lose their balance; and they just went in within a couple of miles of the aerodrome . . .

. . . We eventually became fully night-operational and . . . the whole squadron would be sent up and we'd be stacked up in height. Most of us didn't have much hope of seeing anything unless it was silhouetted between the flames of the burning cities and ourselves and we didn't have much luck – in fact I think the greatest hope we had was an accidental mid-air collision! But we did have one fellow in the squadron who was very successful and that was a fellow called Stevens.[2]

Any lack of success was entirely understandable. The ground controllers could not aid the pilots to anything like the same extent as in daylight. Searchlights and AA guns constantly failed to distinguish friend from foe. The Hurricanes lacked radar, and attempts to use them in combination with American Douglas Havocs which carried an airborne searchlight as well as the AI equipment (but no guns), in spite of being persevered with until early 1943, were almost totally ineffective.

Yet the difficulties, though manifold, were gradually overcome by the pilots' painstaking determination to learn from their mistakes. They trained their eyes by wearing 'dimmer' glasses – goggles with dark lenses – or by keeping away from strong lights at all times. They learned how to use the searchlights and AA bursts as guides to the progress of enemy bombers. Moreover, once they had gained their painful experience, they found that their Hurricanes were easily the most suitable single-engine night-fighters.

The Hurricane in fact enjoyed several valuable advantages in its new role: its fine forward view, its steadiness, its viceless response to control, and, a cynic might add, that wide, sturdy undercarriage which would stand up to the most forceful landing without ill effects. Furthermore it now possessed an improved performance and often a greater firepower as well. The Hurricane Mark II had arrived.

Throughout 1940 the Hawker Design Staff had been investigating the possibilities of providing the Hurricane with a more powerful engine, auxiliary fuel tanks under the wings so as to increase its range, and more machine guns. On 11 June, Philip Lucas took off in an eight-gun Hurricane modified to carry a Merlin XX engine. This gave his machine a top speed of 348 mph which made it the fastest armed Hurricane to fly, and although Hawkers' other plans did not proceed as fast as the development of the Merlin XX, the first Mark IIs reached 111 Squadron in early September.

Known as Mark IIAs Series 1, these aircraft lacked the capacity to carry long-range tanks and had only eight Browning machine guns, but they possessed a top speed of 342 mph, a service ceiling increased to 36,000 feet and a much-improved rate of climb. They were joined a month later by the IIA Series 2 which did have attachment points for either fixed or jettisonable fuel tanks, and over the winter of 1940–41 Hurricane IIAs entered service with a total of eleven squadrons. They in turn were followed by the Hurricane IIB which was armed with twelve Browning machine guns giving it a 50 per cent increase in firepower, in spite of which its performance was almost identical to that of the IIA. By mid-summer twenty Hurricane squadrons were equipped with the IIB version.

Gradually the better performance of the Hurricanes and the greater experience of their pilots began to tell. In January 1941 fighters shot down only three enemy aircraft, in February only four, in both cases considerably less than those brought down by the AA guns. By March, however, the airmen had overtaken the gunners with a figure of twenty-two night raiders destroyed. In April this rose again to forty-eight.

May saw the Luftwaffe's final full-scale night assaults, after which the weight of attacks greatly decreased. It also saw the enemy lose 138 aircraft in various ways, ninety-six of which fell to the night-fighters, a total divided about equally between the RAF's single-engined and twin-engined interceptors. On the night of 10–11 May alone, when a full moon made for unlimited visability, No. 1 Squadron, flying a mixture of Hurricane IIAs and IIBs in the defence of London, was credited with the destruction of seven Heinkel He 111s and one Junkers Ju 88, at the cost of one pilot, killed apparently by AA fire. The Czech Sergeant Dygryn in the course of three sorties personally downed two Heinkels and the Ju 88.

The greatest Hurricane night-fighter pilot during this period, however, was introduced to us earlier: 'a fellow called Stevens'.

Pilot Officer Richard Stevens of 151 Squadron was very different from most of the men who flew Hurricanes. He was older for a start, joining the RAF after the outbreak of war at the age of thirty-two, which was the maximum for pilot training, having flown 400 hours at night as a commercial pilot. Above all he had a personal hatred for the night bombers, which had killed his wife and family in an earlier raid, and he pursued them into the thickest AA fire quite regardless of his own safety and with total ferocity. On one occasion, after blowing up a bomber at point-blank range, he returned with his Hurricane's wings stained by German blood and refused to allow the grisly traces to be removed.

Stevens exacted the first instalment of his vengeance on the night of 15–16 January 1941, when he glimpsed a Dornier Do 17 over London. At once he went in pursuit, and David Masters in *So Few* sets out his account of what happened next:

I picked him up again, climbing at 20,000 feet. He had dropped his bombs and was light. I climbed after him and chased him up to 30,000 feet. Throttling back to cruising speed as I closed, I swung out to make my attack between fifty and twenty-five yards. I saw my ammunition going home and striking him. Bits flew off and hit my aircraft. Oil came back on my windscreen and he just reared straight up. I thought I was going to crash into him, so I turned to one side to get away and only just managed to avoid him. As I did so he went straight down.

Thinking he was trying to fox me, I went down after him flat out from 30,000 to 3,000 feet in a steep spiral. I've never travelled so fast before – you've no idea of speed when you are looking for a Jerry, you just notice when the ground is coming too close and then pull out. I saw him shooting away in a steep climbing turn, so I pulled everything back and did a gentle black-out.[3] Owing to my excess speed I went well outside him and lost him again for a moment. Then I saw him still climbing and quickly closed on him. I gave him a burst from my eight guns and saw little blue flames dancing about his wings and fuselage. At the top of his climb, as he started to stall, I gave him another burst. Flames streamed from him as he went down and crashed at 1:35 am among some trees which he set on fire. Circling round, I climbed to 15,000 feet and went home.

Nor were the adventures of the night over, for when Stevens took off again on a second mission he found a Heinkel He 111 into which he poured a devastating fire. His account goes on to tell us:

He continued to lose height, with both motors smoking. I ran out of ammunition and followed him down to 1,500 feet and then down to 1,000. A little later I lost him over a dark patch of water, so I did not actually see him land.

News was soon forthcoming, however, that Observer posts had confirmed that the Heinkel had crashed – and that Stevens had been awarded an immediate DFC.

Three times more, on 8 April, 10 April and 7 May, Stevens destroyed two enemy aircraft in one night. By November he had gained fourteen night victories – far more than any radar-assisted pilot – and had been promoted to flight lieutenant; he then transferred to another Hurricane squadron, No. 253. On 12 December the award of his DSO was announced. Three nights later, alone as always, he took off on another sortie from which he did not return.

On his last mission Stevens was not defending his country against enemy bombers, he was seeking them out over their own aerodromes as they returned from their raids. It was a characteristic of the Hurricane pilots that they could go from defensive to offensive at a moment's notice and 253 Squadron was far from the only one involved on such intruder missions. As early as the night of 14–15 March 1941, two Hurricanes from 87 Squadron had raided Carpiquet airfield near Caen. In his book *Arise to Conquer*,

Squadron Leader – later Wing Commander – Ian 'Widge' Gleed gives what can only be called an 'action replay':

The [English] coast was a lovely sight, the calm sea reflecting the moon. Every little boat was visible. We climbed slowly upwards. The coast had receded out of sight behind us by the time we were at 12,000 [feet]. It was incredibly lovely looking at the silver sea. After a glance at the instruments, I turned all the cockpit lights out except the compass light. We levelled out at 12,000, and throttled even farther back.

'Christ! There it is' – the 'drome with a square wood at one corner. It looks a terrific light patch: just like its photo that we had seen on the mosaic map [when being briefed]. To the east, a white beacon is blinking the letter B. I throttle back even more. The 'drome, like the town, is completely without lights. Six thousand feet now. Nothing happens. The hangars stand up well, we are still too high to see any aircraft. The huts show up well now. There are about double the number that there had been on the photo. Two thousand feet. There they are. A neat row of twin-engined 'planes; another row. What are they? Junkers 88s. 'Hell! And [Dornier] 215s.' I waggle my wings – the sign for Robbie [Flight Lieutenant Rayner] to break away. At 1,000 feet I shove the throttle full open. That line of about nine will do me nicely. A steep right-hand turn. Now down. Sights on. Steady. I thumb the firing-button. A stream of fire pours from my wings; back on the stick, the line of aircraft flash through my sights. 'Hell! pom-poms.' A string of fiery ping-pong balls tear by my wings; another stream; then another. 'Oh, Hell! searchlights.' Four blue searchlights leap out of the shadows. 'Blast! They've got me.' My wings are suddenly shining a brilliant silver. 'Head in cockpit, quick!' I yank back on the stick. 'Steady. Robbie, pull your finger out and shoot them off me. Thank God I'm clear of them now.' – 'Christ!' a glance behind shows me a stream of pom-pom shells seemingly appearing from a circle round the 'drome, all meeting in an apex. 'Oh God!' For a fleeting second I catch a glimpse of a 'Hurribird' caught in the searchlights surrounded by snacky iridescent shells. 'You bastards!' I pull up into a steep left-hand turn. 'Look out! you'll be coming out of the moon. Oh, blast the moon! Here goes.' I come in low. 'There they are.' Another line of aircraft. Brrrrrrmmmm, brrrmmmmmmmmm. 'Damn those searchlights!' One is shining from straight in front of me. I fly straight at it. Brrrrrmmmmmm, brrrrrm. 'Got you!' For a second there is a red glow, then the searchlight goes out. 'One more dive and I've had enough. Christ, those pompoms are hell.' Brmmmmm, hissssshissssss. 'Blast! Out of ammo. Home, and don't spare the horses.'[4]

The Hurricane pilots continued their night intruder exploits throughout 1941 and well into 1942, destroying enemy warplanes in the air and on the ground, as well as other targets of opportunity. They also succeeded in diverting some of the German night-fighter effort to dealing with them rather than with the heavy bomber raids that the RAF was now mounting – as was gratefully acknowledged by Bomber Command's redoubtable chief, Air Marshal Harris. It may be added that they were assisted in this task by the arrival in the late spring of 1941 of another new Hurricane variant.

This was the Hurricane IIC, the prototype of which first flew on 6 February of that year and which by midsummer was already serving on seven squadrons (including No. 87). Powered by a Merlin XX and armed with four Hispano or Oerlikon cannon – the shells of which, unlike machine-gun bullets, exploded after impact and so provided considerably greater hitting power – the IIC had a maximum speed of 330–336 mph, a service ceiling of 35,600 feet and all the traditional Hurricane virtues of manoeuvrability, reliability and strength.

During 1942 the most successful night intruder squadron was No. 1, equipped with IICs carrying a pair of long-range drop-tanks. Its CO was Squadron Leader James Maclachlan,[5] who has left this description of his own and his squadron's activities:

I must admit that those miles of Channel with only one engine brings mixed thoughts, and one can't help listening to every

66

little beat of the old Merlin as the English coast disappears in the darkness. I always get a feeling of relief and excitement as I cross the French coast and turn on the reflector sight, knowing that anything I can see then I can take a crack at. We have to keep our eyes skinned the whole time, and occasionally glance at the compass and clock. As the minutes go by and we approach the Hun aerodrome, we look eagerly for the flare paths. More often than not we are disappointed. The flare path is switched off as soon as we arrive, and up come the searchlights and flak. But if you're lucky, it's a piece of cake.

The other night [3–4 May 1942] I saw the Jerries when I was still some distance away. They were flying round at about 2,000 feet. I chose the nearest [a Dornier Do 217] and followed him round. He was batting along at about 200 miles an hour, but I soon caught him, and got him beautifully lined up in my sights before letting him have it.

The effect of our four cannon is incredible, after the eight machine-guns I had previously been used to. Scarcely had I pressed the button when a cluster of flashes appeared on the bomber and a spurt of dark red flame came from its starboard engine. The whole thing seemed to fold up then and fall out of the sky, burning beautifully. I turned steeply to watch it crash, and as I did so I saw another Hun about a mile away, coming straight for me. In half a minute he was in my sights, and a second later his port petrol tank was blazing. I gave him another short burst for luck and then flew beside him. It was just like watching a film. A moment before he hit the ground, I could see trees and houses lit up by the dark red glow from the burning machine. Suddenly there was a terrific sheet of flame, and little bits of burning Heinkel flew in all directions.

I was beginning to enjoy myself by this time and flew straight back to the aerodrome to find another. Unfortunately, all the lights had been switched off, and though I circled for some time I found nothing. So I cracked off for home. I looked back once and could still see the two bombers burning in the distance, and a few searchlights trying vainly to find me. On the way back I spotted a train. They're easy to see in the moonlight, as the trail of steam shows up nicely against the dark background. I made sure it was a goods train before attacking the engine, which I left enveloped in a cloud of steam. My squadron has rather specialized in this train-wrecking racket. During the April–May full moon we blew up seventeen engines for certain, and probably several others.[6]

'Train-busting', though, was in the nature of a bonus. No. 1 Squadron's primary objective was savaging the Luftwaffe and during its night intruder missions, which lasted from 1 April 1942 to 2 July 1942, the squadron destroyed twenty-two enemy aircraft, damaging a further thirteen. Maclachlan personally made five of the kills but 1 Squadron's outstanding pilot was the Czech, Flight Lieutenant Karel Kuttelwascher, a brilliant airman and a cool, calculating tactician, who achieved the squadron's earliest success on its very first night of operations. Happily, he later recorded his experiences in a publication called *The Saturday Book* and they are repeated by his biographer (and son-in-law) Roger Darlington in *Night Hawk*:

By dusk everything was ready and, after an hour of waiting in dispersal and a nice cup of English tea, I set off. All the boys wished me luck and told me they would wait in dispersal until I returned. It seemed to me that I had never before in my life taken off so smoothly. I felt so free and exhilarated, with the moon shining above me, and the Channel already in sight. I lowered the revs for economy's sake and with a smoothly purring engine I left the English coast behind me . . .

[Arriving in France] I located . . . [an] aerodrome with its flare path dimmed, and there I saw a plane [a Junkers Ju 88] taxiing with its navigation lights on.

He was just taking off and I swooped down to get beyond him. I passed through his slipstream and got rather a bump but, slowing my speed a little, I was able to get within firing range. With my gun sight and firing button already switched on and the plane looming up right in front of me, I gave it a long burst and saw it catch fire in a matter of seconds. I was obliged to pull out quickly to the right to avoid colliding with it and I watched it hit the ground and burst into flames. I made a half circle to the left and saw just in time another plane taking off. Again I dived, opened fire from slightly above and behind him, but at that moment I was caught by four searchlights and fired on with streams of shells from the ground defences. I had to be content with only damaging this second plane as the firing still continued from the ground. It was not very accurate firing, but it was time for me to make my way home.

Kuttelwascher did even better on 1 Squadron's last night of operations, destroying two enemy aircraft. In between he shot down twelve more. His finest performance of all came on the night of 4–5 May. Again his biographer has given us the Czech's own recollections of his achievement:

Knowing that a large force of enemy planes were attacking England, it was decided that the intruders should go out in strength. We did so and were fully rewarded for our work.

I took off when the attack on one of our towns was finishing. I made my way post-haste to a French aerodrome which I felt sure they must be using for this attack. Some boys had already got there ahead of me, so I hurried to join them at the last minute. What a spectacle confronted me on arriving at the aerodrome . . . About 20 Jerries [Heinkel He 111s] were awaiting their turn to land, and, being in a hurry, they flashed on and off all the lights they had . . .

. . . I decided I had better get within close range and give my victims short bursts in order to make my cannon shells go further. Jerry knew that we were hovering around in strength and so they kept switching their navigation lights on and off to fox us. We, however, went boldly after our prey, knowing that there was no danger from the ground defences while their own planes were flying around. As I was waiting for an opportunity to get at the Jerries, I saw one pass right over my head. In a split second I had pulled my stick back slightly and had fired two short bursts at him. Flames shot instantly out of one engine, and down he went into a steep dive to hit the ground. Again pulling my plane quickly to the right, I did the same to a second one which had been simply begging for it with his navigation lights full on. He too caught fire and hit the ground with a shower of sparks flying all around me.

All this shooting had taken place in one minute, and now I had the opportunity of looking around me a little, as there was nothing in my vicinity at the moment. I saw one of our boys also doing his best and sending a Hun hurtling earthwards in flames. I once more fixed on a Hun to shoot down, but it took me three minutes to get within close range as the devil kept on switching his navigation lights on and off as he waited his turn to land. At last I got into the position for the attack, but this time it took me a little bit more ammo to finish him off. He turned into a steep left hand dive, with me on his tail firing ceaselessly. I was obliged, however, to pull up my plane and climb once more to a safe height as I was too near the ground.

The third Heinkel had duly crashed in flames and since AA guns now began to fire furiously, Kuttelwascher wisely retired. He was rewarded with a DFC soon afterwards.

On 2 July 1942, 1 Squadron stood down from operations and prepared to move north prior to converting to another Hawker fighter, the mighty Typhoon. Kuttelwascher was posted to a Mosquito squadron but he gained no further victories: indeed he never saw another German aircraft. Clearly he had been born to be a Hurricane pilot.

NOTES
1 Not to be confused with Bader's book with the same title. The sub-title of this one is *True Stories of Wartime Fighter Pilots*.
2 Quoted in *Hurricane and Spitfire Pilots at War* by Terence Kelly.
3 So violently did the Hurricane pull out of its dive that the underside of its fuselage was cracked – though seemingly without any ill-effects.
4 Rayner, whose real name was Roderick, though Gleed calls him 'Robbie', also returned safely.
5 Maclachlan was a veteran Hurricane pilot having previously flown with 261 Squadron in Malta, where he gained two victories before

being shot down on 2 February 1941 with his left arm so shattered by a cannon shell that it had to be amputated above the elbow. Fitted with an artificial limb, he returned to operations first with 73 Squadron in North Africa, then with 1 Squadron.

6 This account first appeared as a radio broadcast but was later collected with others by the Ministry of Information for the Air Ministry and published under the title *Over to You*.

Chapter 6

Action in the Arctic

Apart from the growing effectiveness of the defences, the main reason why the night bombing of Britain had fallen away after May 1941 was that the Luftwaffe's attentions had been directed elsewhere. On 22 June, Hitler hurled his legions against Russia and although the vast distances involved and the early arrival of 'General Winter' prevented their obtaining a victory similar to that won in France, they at first sent their opponents reeling back with terrible losses of men and material.

On learning that Britain had a new ally, Churchill at once promised Russia everything that could be spared in the way of aid. In August the two countries jointly occupied Iran in order to secure a supply route to Russia through the Middle East, over which five million tons of arms, aircraft and ammunition would eventually pass. So too would military vehicles: in the period from August 1944 to April 1945 alone nearly half-a-million of them, sufficient to enable the Red Army to equip sixty motorized divisions.

Because it took time to improve the Iranian transport system, however, this route became fully effective only in 1943. Before then the bulk of the aid had to make the perilous journey through the Arctic Ocean round the North Cape of Norway to the ice-free Russian port of Murmansk, 200 miles to the east at the head of the Kola Inlet, or to Archangel a further 400 miles to the south-east where the unloading facilities were vastly better but where even the strenuous attempts of the

72

Russian ice-breakers were unable to keep the port open during the months of winter.

In all forty convoys would dare the Arctic run. They carried a total of four million tons of cargo, though 300,000 tons of this would be lost en route. By the end of May 1942 they had already delivered 3,000 aircraft, 4,000 tanks, 30,000 other vehicles, 42,000 tons of petrol, 66,000 tons of fuel oil and 800,000 tons of miscellaneous supplies including food, ammunition, machine-tools, medical equipment and such raw materials as rubber, aluminium and tin. In view of the vast scale of the conflict on the Eastern Front, the weapons were perhaps less significant than might have appeared at first sight, but the motor transport was of immense importance to judge by the extent to which it formed the equipment of the Red Army by the end of the war, and the raw materials were even more vital as without them the Russians could not have manufactured hardened steel or certain special alloys.

During the first months of hostilities the Russians lost immense numbers of aircraft, so every aeroplane supplied must also have been of outstanding value. It was decided that the first batch would be Hurricanes which had already proved their ability to operate in Arctic conditions in Norway and were also being shipped to Iceland at this time to protect the British garrison there. Meanwhile Finland had sought revenge for an unprovoked Russian attack in 1939 by allying with Germany and had given the Luftwaffe bases within close range of Murmansk and Archangel. It was determined therefore to send an advance force to Russia which could help defend those ports and at the same time teach the Russians how to fly and maintain their new acquisitions when these arrived.

Accordingly at the end of August the very first convoy set out for Russia. Preceding even the famous PQ convoys, as they were called from their code numbers – returning convoys naturally enough were coded QP – it carried 151 Wing which had only come into being on 12 August under Wing Commander Ramsbottom-Isherwood who was a New Zealander, but whose family, surely, had originally hailed from the North Country. The Wing contained two new Hurricane squadrons, No. 81 led by Squadron

Leader Rook and No. 134 under Squadron Leader Miller. They were equipped mainly with IIBs, plus a handful of IIAs, twenty-four of their aircraft travelling on the little aircraft carrier HMS *Argus*, while fifteen more in crates, together with the ground crews, were on board the seven accompanying merchantmen, the main cargoes of which were munitions.

On 7 September the pilots took off from *Argus* for Vaenga airfield, some 17 miles from Murmansk. The merchant ships were diverted to Archangel but the other fifteen Hurricanes were quickly assembled here. They and the remaining Wing personnel then rejoined their companions at Vaenga, where a surface of rolled sand, combined with frequent bad weather, gave the Hurricanes numerous opportunities to prove their ruggedness.

They soon proved their effectiveness as well. On 12 September a flight of Hurricanes from 81 Squadron sighted a Henschel Hs 126 reconnaissance machine, suitably protected by Messerschmitt Bf 109s. Though they were then armed only with six machine guns each to reduce weight for their flight from *Argus*, the Hurricanes attacked at once, damaging the Henschel and shooting down three of the 109s for the loss of Sergeant Smith, who as it transpired, would be the only pilot to be killed during the Wing's stay in Russia.

One of the victors on this occasion was Flight Sergeant – later Squadron Leader – Charlton 'Wag' Haw whose Combat Report is set out in *Hawker Hurricane* by Peter Jacobs:

Whilst leading a patrol of Hurricanes over the enemy lines I intercepted five Bf 109s escorting a Hs 126. My height was 3,500 ft. The enemy aircraft were approaching from ahead and slightly to the left, and as I turned towards them, they turned slowly to the right. I attacked the leader and as he turned I gave him a ten second burst from the full beam position. The enemy aircraft rolled on to its back and as it went down it burst into flames. I did not see it crash owing to taking evasive action but Red 2 [Pilot Officer Walker] confirms that it crossed him in a 70-degree dive at 500 ft, smoke and flames still pouring from it.

On 17 September 81 Squadron's Hurricanes, by now carrying their full armament of twelve machine guns, were again in action. German ground troops were beginning to threaten Murmansk and were consequently coming under attack by Russian bombers. On this occasion the squadron was detailed to cover the bombers as they returned from a raid, though in future the Hurricanes would fly with them as close escort. In *The Hawker Hurricane*, Francis K. Mason sets out the appropriate entry from the Squadron Diary:

> At 1855 hours eight Bf 109Es were intercepted when about to attack the Russian bombers. The C.O. [Squadron Leader Rook] attacked a Bf 109E with a two-second burst, hitting the radiator, and chased it for about five minutes using up all his ammunition. After further attacks by Sgt Sims and Sgt Anson the enemy aircraft crashed. Sgt Anson was then attacked by Russian fighters and had to take evasive action. F/Sgt Haw made a stern attack on a Bf 109E without visible effect but after a three-second burst from a quarter-attack at 150 yards the enemy caught fire. Plt Off Bush out-turned another Bf 109, setting it on fire with a two-second burst; after another short burst the enemy aircraft crashed.

It is clear from this that Flight Sergeant Haw had once again downed an enemy aircraft. In his Combat Report, repeated by Peter Jacobs in *Hawker Hurricane*, he adds some interesting details. The first part merely echoes the observations in the Squadron Diary, which no doubt were derived from it, but Haw then continues:

> During this attack smoke began to pour from the enemy aircraft, a large piece flew off him and he rolled onto his back and went into a vertical dive. An enemy pilot who baled out was identified by the Russian Observer Corps as being the pilot of the machine which I attacked. The piece of the enemy aircraft which flew off was probably the hood being jettisoned.

Whatever the exact circumstances, Haw had destroyed his second 109 in Russia and he would later add a third, to make him the highest-scoring pilot in 151 Wing. By 27 November, with its tasks completed, the Wing, apart from a small staff of signals personnel, sailed for home and Peter Jacobs appropriately ends his account of Haw's exploits with a signal received on that date from the Commander of the Soviet Northern Fleet:

> To Pilot of the Royal 'Military' Air Fleet of Great Britain, SERGEANT HAW C.E.
> I congratulate you with the High Government award of the Union of Socialist Republics, the 'Order of Lenin'. Your manliness, heroism and excellent mastery of battles of the air have always assured victory over the enemy. I wish you new victories in battles against the common enemy of all progressive nations, ie – German fascism.
> Signed Vice-Admiral A. Golovko.

Haw also received a less glamorous British decoration, the Distinguished Flying Medal. He appears to have thought this entirely adequate.

In all during its stay in Russia, 81 Squadron shot down twelve enemy aircraft, including three of the new improved versions of the Messerschmitt, the Bf 109F. Each victory incidentally brought with it a bonus of 100 roubles, then worth about £20, but the airmen's jests that this would infringe their 'amateur status' merely masked a distaste for such 'blood money' – which ultimately went to the RAF Benevolent Fund. That 81 Squadron's claims were by no means exaggerated can be seen from this report, appearing in Maurice Allward's *Hurricane Special*, by Flight Lieutenant Hubert Griffith, 151 Wing's adjutant:

> Late one afternoon, 'B' Flight, 81 Squadron, had come down from a patrol, claiming three victories. Two of these were unquestionable. There was no possible doubt about them. They had been seen by independent witnesses to crash into the ground, and the wrecks had been identified. About the third there was a dispute. The young Scottish pilot who had

engaged the third aircraft swore that he had got to close quarters, had squirted his 12 guns into it in a long close-range burst of fire, and had only desisted when he had seen the enemy machine go down in an out-of-control spin in a cloud near the ground. His story was confirmed, in detail, by his flight commander, a pilot of long experience. But it was the Squadron Leader, a pilot of even greater experience, who had to give the decision on what claim to put in to Intelligence, and his comment on hearing the story was: 'Yes . . . but they can take an awful lot of lead and still get away with it; we'll only have to claim him a "probable".'

The encounter then was entered in the records as a 'probable', and the matter could have finished there. It was only the next morning, when the wreckage of the third enemy machine had been definitely identified on the ground, that the claim was allowed to go forward as a certain victory.

134 Squadron was less successful, due partly to sheer bad luck. It flew offensive patrols and took its turn in escorting Russian bombers, but the only time it saw action was when enemy aircraft delivered a raid of their own on Vaenga. Flight Lieutenant Jack Ross notes the affair all too briefly in his diary which appears in Chaz Bowyer's *Hurricane at War*:

Oct 6th.
Aerodrome attacked by 14 Ju 88s, escorted by 109s, while A Flight was practice flying. [Pilot Officer] Cameron two damaged; [Pilot Officer] Furneaux ½ confirmed (with Rook); [Sergeant] Barnes and [Pilot Officer] Elkington one confirmed. F/Lt Rook [a cousin of 81's C.O.] one Me 109 confirmed. Several more damaged. B Flight aircraft took off during bombing. Aerodrome machine-gunned at same time.

Another reason for 134 Squadron's comparative lack of success was that it was mainly responsible for training Russian pilots to fly Hurricanes. General Kuznetsov was the first to take up the Hawker fighter, followed quickly by Captains Safanov and

Kuharenko. The fact that two Hurricanes were crashed by the Russians – though both were repairable – is scarcely surprising when the enthusiastic outlook of the pupils is taken into account. They would demand training even in the most appalling conditions. One of them is reported to have taken off in a Hurricane for the first time in the middle of a snowstorm. That he landed safely is a tribute to both man and machine.

With training completed and with an almost total absence of daylight at Vaenga, which was 170 miles north of the Arctic Circle, bringing activities almost to a standstill, both RAF squadrons handed over their machines to the 72nd Regiment of the Red Naval Air Fleet. Reinforced by other Hurricanes which had now arrived on the early Arctic convoys, they were formed by Safanov, newly promoted to colonel, into the first Russian Hurricane Wing. It was the first of many, for from 1941 to 1944, 2,952 Hurricanes left for Russia, though in view of the losses suffered by the convoys, many undoubtedly disappeared en route.

Of those aircraft supplied of which details are known, at least 210 were IIAs, 1,557 were IIBs and 1,009 IICs. They were employed mainly on orthodox fighter duties, though several were converted into two-seaters for use as advanced trainers. After the war Hawkers produced a similar version for the Persian Air Force, and it seems probable that the adaptation would have proved a singularly happy one since the Hurricane's mixture of strength and docility made it ideal for such a role.

Unfortunately for propaganda purposes the Soviet authorities tended to decry the value of the aid received from Britain, and later from the United States, though their own angry protests when deliveries were postponed for any reason are sufficient to demonstrate their falsehood. They therefore preferred to suppress almost all references to Hurricanes, being content to grumble that too few were handed over. Just occasionally though, a gleam of light is thrown on their achievements – for example in the 'Soviet War News' issue of 3 October 1942, which is set out in Maurice Allward's *Hurricane Special*:

Then a batch of English Hawker Hurricane fighters arrived at the Front. The speeds for which these machines are designed suggested that they would be particularly suitable as escorts for the Ilyushin bombers. Their excellent lateral manoeuvrability promised a solution to the problem of low-level fighters. It was therefore decided to employ Hurricanes to escort the Il bombers. For about three months now Major Gorshkov's unit of Hurricanes has been escorting your fighter-bombers on their sorties. His airmen have splendid victories to their credit.

On one occasion six Hurricanes were detailed to accompany eight Il aircraft. The Group Leader, Lieutenant Dobrovolsky, decided against dividing his forces, preferring to keep them in the immediate vicinity of the bombers, the better to ensure their protection. Over the target they were met by eight Messerschmitts. The bombers were flying at an altitude of 1,300 feet, and they immediately formed into a circle. Among them the Hurricanes were busy keeping the enemy busy. After a few minutes, Dobrovolsky set fire to one Messerschmitt, then Sergeants Barishnyov and Bunakov each made a kill. While this fight was going on, the bombers, without breaking their circle, continued to strafe the troop concentrations. When they ran out of bombs they veered round in a wide sweep and started on their return journey. This fight ended in the complete defeat of the German airmen, who, after losing three of their aircraft, were forced to give up the attack. Such tactics are now common practice among Soviet pilots and they have brought excellent results. In three months' hard work, the Il bombers have suffered one loss from attacks by enemy fighters. The quality of the Hurricane has made it possible for us to solve the important problem of ensuring the safety of the Il.

The British machines have proved equally successful on reconnaissance duty and in guarding troops and military objectives. For over two months past, Major Panov's unit has been flying Hurricanes. With some 20 machines at his disposal, his unit has brought down 83 German planes in aerial combat, including 31 bombers, and this for the price of only four pilots and ten planes.

Since descriptions for the Hurricane in action over Russia are so rare, it is worth analyzing this one a bit further. During this same period, Hurricanes were proving very effective escorting Allied bombers in North Africa. Restricted as they were by the need to protect their charges, they sometimes suffered heavy casualties of their own from attacking 109s but these were hardly ever able to break past the escorts to engage their much more vital targets. For that matter Hurricanes had already proved their worth on escort duties in Russia at the time of 151 Wing's visit. It was said then that the Soviet bomber crews had such faith in the protection provided by the Hurricanes that they went straight for their targets without even bothering to look overhead. The statement no doubt contained an element of exaggeration but the Russians had every reason to feel confident in their escorts – in the course of the thirty-five or so strikes guarded by 151 Wing's Hurricanes, a single bomber was lost to AA fire but not one to enemy fighters.

There seems then no reason to doubt that Major Gorshkov's unit did enjoy great success in protecting the Ilyushins, especially as it is admitted that this was not (quite) a 100 per cent one. As regards the specific action recounted, three enemy fighters destroyed without loss was a good but not spectacular achievement and it is to be noted that the victorious pilots are named. This therefore also rings true – though there may well have been other less successful exchanges which the 'Soviet War News' tactfully omits.

Nor is there any reason to doubt that the Hurricane was 'equally successful' in the reconnaissance role. This is not a task with which the Hurricane is normally associated but again it carried out such duties with great effect in North Africa, its armament being reduced to only two machine guns at the most in order to save weight.

Only the claims of Major Panov's unit are entitled to raise genuine doubts, for there can be no question that Russian pilots like those of every other country, did overestimate the damage they had caused, duplicate successes and generally exaggerate their achievements. Even so it does seem that this unit was enjoying a high degree of success. That only ten Hurricanes were lost can well be accepted, knowing the ruggedness of the type, though there were probably some others which returned to base in a somewhat battered condition. So can the loss of only four pilots – it has already been shown that the majority of Hurricane pilots escaped with their lives even when their machines were brought down.

It is interesting to note that the Hurricane was still gaining victories in the pure fighter role in Russia in late 1942. It was now hardly ever used as such on the Channel Front where the RAF was committed to offensive sweeps. Its speed had reached its limit and its still 'excellent' manoeuvrability was less valuable for operations in enemy airspace where it would have to stop manoeuvring eventually in order to fly home. By contrast the Germans were still on the attack in Russia, as they were for much of this time in North Africa, and in both areas the Hurricane was more than capable of fighting defensive campaigns – 'guarding troops and military objectives' for instance.

By early 1943 though, the Hurricanes in Russia (and North Africa) had joined those in Britain in being used almost entirely for ground-attack duties. The IICs with their 20-mm cannon are said to have proved particularly effective against German motor transport and they clearly awoke in the Russians a desire for Hurricanes with still more powerful weapons, as witness this message from Stalin to Churchill dated 12 April 1943:

The contemplated deliveries of fighters . . . are of great value to us. I am also very grateful for your offer to send us sixty Hurricanes armed with 40-mm cannon. Such planes are very needed, especially against heavy tanks.

The Hurricanes with the 40-mm cannon were known as Mark IIDs and were specifically designed for the anti-tank role; more will be written of them in due course. The sixty mentioned were duly dispatched, as were at least thirty Mark IVs, an all-purpose close-support version, which will also be described in more detail later. It seems reasonable to suggest that they proved even more valuable than the IICs in the ground-attack role, for which they had been especially created.

From such information as is available, it also seems reasonable to suggest that the Hurricane played a not unworthy part in the titanic struggles on the Eastern Front. It must be a matter of lasting regret that political bigotry should have ensured that the stories of perhaps one-fifth of the men who flew Hurricanes can never now be told.

Chapter 7

Action over the Med

From the Mediterranean theatre, on the other hand, come numerous accounts of Hurricane pilots' exploits. Nor do they come only from airmen, for it was in this theatre that the Hurricane led the way to that co-ordination between the Royal Air Force and the British Army which would bring about their country's most spectacular triumphs.

When the Italian dictator Benito Mussolini entered the war on 10 June 1940, there were just two Hurricanes in the Middle East. Both were added to the strength of 80 Squadron, one of them, which had been shipped out to Egypt a short time previously, claiming the Hurricane's first victims in this new conflict when Flying Officer Wykeham-Barnes shot down two Fiat CR 42 biplane fighters on the 19th.

The other Hurricane was unable to take such an active part. It had been sent to the Sudan at the end of 1939 to test the tropical filter which had to be fitted over the Hurricane's carburettor air intake to protect the Merlin engine from dust or sand particles. When it joined 80 Squadron in July 1940 its guns had been rendered inoperative by the hostile environment, but it still made its presence felt by flying from landing ground to landing ground in an attempt to convince the Italians that large numbers of modern fighters were reaching North Africa. It seems that the bluff worked; certainly the Regia Aeronautica appeared by no means eager to venture over the British lines.

On the occasions that it did, it was met by a slowly increasing number of Hurricanes. Before the fall of France about fifty were sent to North Africa through France, Tunisia and Malta, though the flights were made to the limits of the Hurricane's range and only a handful reached their destination and joined 80 Squadron. This had now been entrusted with protecting Admiral Cunningham's Mediterranean Fleet. On 17 August Flying Officer Lapsley provided admirable protection by shooting down three Savoia Marchetti SM 79 bombers, all of them confirmed in enemy records.

Two days later, 80 Squadron gave up its Hurricanes to form the nucleus of a new squadron, No. 274. Its CO, Squadron Leader Dunn, took over this unit and several of his pilots with experience on Hurricanes joined him, including Lapsley who on 10 September gained 274 Squadron's first successes by downing two more SM 79s despite damage to his own aircraft. In addition, more Hurricanes were shipped across the Mediterranean in crates – though this route was becoming more perilous almost daily – and these were used to equip 33 Squadron.

Meanwhile the Italian ground forces, which greatly out-numbered those of the British Empire and Commonwealth, were pushing rather hesitantly into British or British-protected terri-tories. From the Italian colony of Libya in North Africa they made a strictly limited advance into Egypt. From East Africa where the Italian colonies of Eritrea and Italian Somaliland flanked Abyssinia, a picturesque but backward country swallowed up by Mussolini in 1936, they seized some frontier posts in the Sudan and Kenya and forced the evacuation of British Somaliland which, surrounded as it was by hostile territory, was totally indefensible.

Fortunately the Italians were neither mentally prepared nor properly equipped for modern warfare. The British Commander-in-Chief, Middle East, General Sir Archibald Wavell, realized this and with astonishing audacity ordered his subordinate comman-ders, O'Connor in Egypt, Platt in the Sudan and Cunningham in Kenya, to take the offensive. The first such attack, against frontier posts on the Sudan-Abyssinian border, was launched on 6 November. Complete surprise was obtained, numbers for once were roughly equal, the British had tanks which the Italians lacked, the officer in command was Brigadier Slim who later led the

1a. Early Hurricanes of 111 Squadron, the first to receive the type in December 1937.

1b. Early Hurricane pilots. *Left:* Wing Commander Roland Beamont who as a young pilot officer flew Hurricanes with 87 Squadron during the Battle of France and the Battle of Britain; *centre:* Flying Officer Edgar 'Cobber' Kain of 73 Squadron who became one of the first RAF 'aces' – he is shown with his fiancée the repertory actress Joyce Phillips; *right:* Wing Commander 'Pat' Jameson, a flight lieutenant with 46 Squadron during the ill-fated Norwegian campaign.

1c. Hurricanes coming in to land on a French airfield.

2. Variations on a theme. Pilots race to their Hurricanes. *Top:* 87 Squadron in France; *bottom:* 601 Squadron during the Battle of Britain.

3a. Sergeant James 'Ginger' Lacey had long lost the belief that he would never be able to fly a Hurricane by the time this photo of him in the cockpit of one was taken. He was then a squadron leader and had become the RAF's top-scoring pilot by the end of the Battle of Britain.

3b. Sergeant Josef Frantisek, the Czech who flew with 303 (Polish) Squadron and who at the time of his tragic death in a landing accident had gained more victories than anyone else during the Battle of Britain.

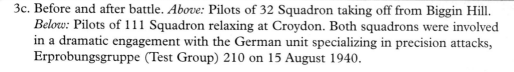

3c. Before and after battle. *Above:* Pilots of 32 Squadron taking off from Biggin Hill. *Below:* Pilots of 111 Squadron relaxing at Croydon. Both squadrons were involved in a dramatic engagement with the German unit specializing in precision attacks, Erprobungsgruppe (Test Group) 210 on 15 August 1940.

4. More Hurricane pilots who fought in the Battle of Britain. *Top left:* Group Captain 'Max' Aitken who was C.O. of 601 Squadron at the start of the battle and had earlier gained victories in both day and night encounters. *Top right:* Sub Lieutenant 'Dickie' Cork, a Fleet Air Arm officer who joined Douglas Bader's 242 Squadron during the Battle and later played a distinguished part in the passage of the Malta Convoy Operation PEDESTAL. *Bottom left:* Bader himself *(centre)* with two of his pilots. On the left of the picture is Flying Officer 'Willie' McKnight; on the right, Flight Lieutenant Eric Ball. Bottom right: Flight Lieutenant (later Wing Commander) James Brindley Nicholson who won fighter Command's only Victoria Cross on 16 August 1940.

5. Men and Machines. *Top:* Squadron Leader (later Wing Commander) Robert Stanford Tuck in a Hurricane of 257 'Burma' Squadron. *Middle:* Arthur 'Taffy' Clowes with his Hurricane. A flying officer at the time this photo was taken, Clowes rose from sergeant to flight lieutenant in No. 1 Squadron before becoming CO of another Hurricane squadron, No. 79. He was later a wing commander. *Bottom left:* Close-up of Tuck and 257's squadron badge. *Bottom right:* Close-up of Clowes and the wasp emblem on his Hurricane. He added a new stripe to it every time he gained another victory.

6a. Hurricanes of 85 Squadron towards the end of the Battle of Britain.

6b. Pilots of 85 Squadron towards the end of the Battle of Britain. Squadron Leader Peter Townsend still carries a stick as a result of a wound in the foot received on 31 August 1940.

6c. Hurricane night-fighter pilots. *Left:* Sergeant 'Doug' Nicholls of 151 Squadron. (He would later reach the rank of squadron leader.) *Right:* 'Mac' and 'Kut', Squadron Leader James Maclachlan and Flight Lieutenant Karel Kuttelwascher, No. Squadron's night intruder experts.

7a. Squadron Leader Ian 'Widge' Gleed, CO of 87 Squadron with his mascot 'Figaro'.

7b. Unusual shot of Flight Lieutenant 'Roddy' Rayner (at this time a pilot officer during the Battle of Britain) who flew as Gleed's No. 2 during the intruder raid on Carpiquet airfield on the night of 14/15 March 1941.

7c. 87 Squadron's Hurricanes were painted black for their night-fighter activities.

8. They All Flew Hurricanes; four different men who saw service in four different areas, but all in the same type of aircraft.

Top left: Major James Goodson, one of many American citizens who joined the RAF as volunteers and were stationed at airfields in Britain.

Top right: Squadron Leader (later Group Captain) John Simpson is shown here in a Hurricane of 245 Squadron stationed in Northern Ireland, but he had earlier helped to cover the evacuation of Allied forces from France.

Bottom left: Flying Officer (later Air Vice-Marshal) John Lapsley in a Hurricane of 80 Squadron which took part in the early campaigns in North Africa.

Bottom right: Sergeant Terence Kelly of 258 Squadron who saw much action in Sumatra and Java.

9a. 151 Wing in Russia. *Top:* a Hurricane IIB of 81 Squadron; *bottom:* IIB of 134 Squadron.

9b. Hurricane pilots who fought in Russia: *Left to right:* Captain Boris Safanov who received rapid promotion to colonel and took over 151 Squadron's aircraft to form the basis of the first Russian Hurricane Wing; Squadron Leader (later Wing Commander) 'Tony' Rook, CO of 81 Squadron; Flight Sergeant (later Squadron Leader) Charlton 'Wag' Haw, also of 81 Squadron, who was the Wing's top scorer in Russia.

10. South African Activities. *Above:* Captain (later Major) John 'Jack' Frost, 3 Squadron SAAF's most successful pilot of the East African campaigns, climbs into his Hurricane. *Right:* Major Gerald 'Lemmie' Le Mesurier who flew with 1 Squadron SAAF during the East African campaigns and later commanded it in some of the hardest-fought campaigns in North Africa. *Bottom:* Hurricanes of 1 Squadron SAAF over the Sudan, close to the border with Eritrea.

11a. Hurricanes – the shadows show there were five of them – taking off from a landing-ground in North Africa.

11b. Squadron Leader M.T. St J. 'Pat' Pattle who as CO of 33 Squadron and earlier as a flight lieutenant in 80 Squadron became the RAF's top scoring fighter 'ace'.

11c. Flying Officer (later Squadron Leader) William 'Cherry' Vale of 80 Squadron who was the RAF's most successful pilot in the fighting over Crete.

12a. Sergeant 'Fred' Robertso[n]
had an unfortunate arriv[al]
in Malta at the conclusio[n]
of Operation HURRY b[ut]
subsequently became on[e]
of the island's most value[d]
defenders.

12b. Hurricane of 261 Squadron on Malta.

12c. Sea Hurricane IBs on an aircraft carrier in 1942. These were the fighters that
defended the crucial Malta convoys in the summer of that year.

13a. Sea Hurricane IA. *Top:* Being hoisted on to the catapult of a CAM-ship. *Bottom:* Being launched from the catapult.

13b. Hurricane IIB fighter-bomber being prepared for a cross-Channel sortie.

13c. Hurricane IV mounting two 40mm anti-tank guns.

14a. Hurricane pilots who fought in North Africa. *Left:* The Canadian George Keefer was a squadron leader at the time this picture was taken and he later became a wing commander, but he served as a flight lieutenant with 274 Squadron during most of the North African campaigns. *Centre:* Squadron Leader (later Group Captain) Michael Stephens CO of 80 Squadron at the time of Operation CRUSADER. *Right:* Wing Commander (later Group Captain) Michael Pedley who led 43 Squadron to Algiers immediately following the successful Alllied landings – Operation TORCH.

14b. Hurricanes that fought in North Africa. *Top left:* Anti-tank Hurricane IIDs of No. 6 Squadron. *Top right:* Close-up of the IID's 40mm cannon. *Bottom left:* Hurricane IIB fighter-bomber. This one is shown at a maintenance unit but the type saw action throughout almost all the fighting in North Africa. *Bottom right:* Hurricane IIC of 213 Squadron at El Alamein. It was the aircraft of this squadron, together with those of 238, which in November 1942 carried out the innocently named Operation CHOCOLATE.

15a. Rocket-armed Hurricane IVs of No. 6 Squadron at Prkos, Yugoslavia.

15b. Hurricane taking off from the Red Road airstrip, Calcutta.

15c. Hurricane pilots who fought in Burma. *Left:* Gordon Conway was a flight lieutenant when this picture was taken and later became a wing commander, but he arrived at the India-Burma front as a young pilot officer with 136 Squadron; he would see a great deal of action in the first half of 1943. *Right:* Flight Lieutenant 'Denny' Sharp who was soon to become CO of No. 11 Squadron.

16a. Hurricane IIDs of 20 Squadron 'looking for trouble' off the coast of Burma.

16b. 'Hurribomber' being prepared for action on a Burmese airfield.

16c. 'Hurribomber' in action: attacking a target in Burma.

Fourteenth Army in Burma – and with all these advantages the assault was thrown back amidst circumstances of disgraceful panic.

The reason for this humiliation was simple. The Italians had command of the air. First, CR 42s drove away the protective cover of Gladiators, to which they were superior in numbers and performance, shooting down five of them without loss. Then the Italian bombers pounded the ground troops with accuracy and zeal. It was clear that Hurricanes were desperately needed – but how would it be possible to get a regular supply of them to the Middle East?

The answer, it transpired, lay in West Africa. Later, Hurricanes would be sent to Sierra Leone and Gambia to defend their ports, but the crucial port in 1940 was Takoradi in what was then the Gold Coast. Here a Maintenance Unit was set up by Group Captain Thorold, to which Hurricanes would be shipped, usually in a dismantled condition. They would be reassembled, fitted with long-range tanks and then, guided by twin-engined aircraft, they would set off for Egypt by way of a series of staging posts.

The perils of the flight are graphically described in the RAF Official History:

The first stage, 378 miles of humid heat diversified by sudden squalls, followed the palm-fringed coast to Lagos, with a possible halt at Accra. Next came 525 miles over hill and jungle to an airfield of red dust outside Kano, after which 325 miles of scrub, broken by occasional groups of mud houses, would bring the aircraft to Maiduguri. A stretch of hostile French territory some 650 miles wide,[1] consisting largely of sand, marsh, scrub and rocks, would then beguile the pilot's interest until he reached El Geneina, in the Anglo-Egyptian Sudan. Here, refreshed with the knowledge that he had covered nearly half of his journey, he would contemplate with more equanimity the 200 miles of mountain and burning sky which lay between him and El Fasher. A brief refuelling halt, with giant cacti providing a pleasing variety in the vegetation, and in another 560 miles the wearied airman might brave the disapproving glances of immaculate figures in khaki and

85

luxuriate for a few hours in the comforts of Khartoum. Thence, with a halt at Wadi Halfa, where orange trees and green gardens contrast strangely with the desert, and a house built by Gordon and used by Kitchener shelters the passing traveller, he had only to fly down the Nile a thousand miles to Abu Sueir. When he got there his airmanship would doubtless be all the better for the flight. Not so, however, his aircraft.

Not so in particular his aircraft's engine. As already mentioned, the Hurricanes in the Middle East carried a tropical filter to protect their engines and this reduced the speed and rate of climb, particularly of the Mark I, but of the Mark II as well. Pilots who flew Hurricanes in both Britain and the Middle East have said that the 'tropical' versions were like carthorses compared to thoroughbreds. Nonetheless the filter had to be adopted as the alternative was the rapid destruction of the engine. Nor was this the only problem faced by Hurricanes operating in the Western Desert of Egypt and Libya. Wind-driven sand caused such wear on their canopy perspex that in time this would become almost opaque and led to some pilots risking a buffeting from the wind and flying without canopies altogether. The Germans incidentally were not so handicapped as their perspex was of a higher quality.

In any case the Hurricanes had to get to the Western Desert first. On 27 November thirty-four Hurricanes of the already famous 73 Squadron flew off the deck of the carrier *Furious* at Takoradi. One crashed into the sea, though the pilot was rescued unhurt. The others set off over the supply route but on 1 December the Blenheim leading the first six lost its way on the flight to El Fasher. All seven machines crash-landed in the desert, two of the Hurricanes were written off and one pilot was killed. When the remaining twenty-seven reached Egypt they still had to be checked, provided with guns which had been removed to save weight, and stripped of their long-range tanks.

Nonetheless by mid-December the Takoradi route had provided enough Hurricanes to bring 33 and 274 Squadrons up to full strength and to begin providing 208 Squadron with Tac R

(Tactical Reconnaissance) Hurricanes, fitted with a forward-facing camera, to replace its Lysanders. Moreover the first twelve aircraft of 73 Squadron were also ready for action, the squadron's most expert pilot during this early period being Sergeant Marshall who specialized in bringing down Savoia Marchetti SM 79s: two on 16 December, three more on 3 January 1941, and a sixth the following day.

These victories were gained while the Hurricanes were supporting the British Western Desert Force which in a dramatic assault starting on 9 December first drove the Italians out of Egypt, then invaded Libya's eastern province of Cyrenaica. Its triumphant progress owed much to the fact that by mid-January the Hurricanes had achieved complete aerial supremacy. Not only were the Italian airmen quite unable to harm the Allied soldiers, but their own troops were under constant attack from the RAF in general and the Hurricanes in particular. Alan Moorehead, the Australian war correspondent, accompanied the victorious advance and in his book *The Desert War* he gives numerous illustrations of Hurricane pilots in action:

> Hurricanes flying only thirty or forty feet above the ground were ranging back and forth over the whole of eastern Cyrenaica, blowing up staff cars and transports, machine-gunning troops and gathering information of the movements of the enemy. By the time Tobruk fell, the Italian air force was utterly defeated, and it was never afterwards restored to superiority . . .
>
> [The RAF] had concentrated on damaging enemy aircraft on the ground by low-level machine-gun attacks. This put the enemy machines out of action long enough to enable our troops to come up and seize the airfields. Around Tobruk I had already seen nearly a hundred aircraft caught in this way . . .
>
> . . . In that hectic three weeks between the fall of Tobruk and the taking of Benghazi the Italians were never given a moment's rest. Through every daylight hour Hurricanes were swooping on them at three hundred miles an hour, or the Blenheims were bombing . . .

[At Derna] a staid, slow flight of Savoias – the last we were to see – had been over bombing until it ran into a lone Hurricane coming back from patrol into Libya. The Australians forgot the shelling, forgot momentarily the wounded nearby and their hunger, and raised a cheer as the Hurricane dived straight through the Italian machines and sent one dropping with that breath-taking fateful slowness to the red desert. Its bursting flames rose from behind the wreckage of the other broken aircraft on the [air]field . . .

[At Benghazi] Hurricanes had just passed that way making a frightful wreckage on the road where they had caught and overturned several lorries full of men. The vehicles were uprooted bodily from the track, and the unwounded passengers frantically waved white handkerchiefs at us as we passed by.

By 7 February 1941, the whole of Cyrenaica was in British hands and the Italian Army had been trapped and forced to surrender. It was a magnificent victory, made greater by the successes that were taking place in East Africa at the same time, and in which again Hurricanes performed a crucial service. The Allied advance from the Sudan into Eritrea was aided by the Hurricanes of 1 Squadron South African Air Force which protected the soldiers most effectively and, as in Cyrenaica, destroyed large numbers of Italian aircraft on their aerodromes as well as attacking the Italian ground forces. By early April all Eritrea had been overrun, an achievement not only welcome in itself but, since the Italians' finest troops had been sent to Eritrea, one which paved the way for a still more spectacular advance from Kenya.

This, directed at first against Italian Somaliland, was supported by the Hurricanes of 3 Squadron SAAF. One of its pilots, Captain Frost, won a DFC by destroying four enemy machines in one day on 3 February 1941, but once more the Hurricanes were particularly effective against Italian aircraft on the ground. With air supremacy gained, Italian Somaliland was occupied by the end of February and the British and Commonwealth troops struck into Abyssinia from the south, their way again being cleared by Hurricane strikes on enemy aerodromes. On 15 March, during such an attack at Diredawa, Captain Frost was forced to crash-land, but Lieutenant Kershaw landed voluntarily and his Hurricane took off safely with Frost sitting on his knees – a feat for which Kershaw was awarded a DSO. On 6 April Addis Ababa, capital of Abyssinia, fell, and thereafter the remaining pockets of Italian resistance were steadily mopped up until the surrender of the last, at Gondar, on 28 November.

Yet in one sense the Hurricanes' triumphs had been too complete, as Lapsley – who would rise to the rank of Air Vice-Marshal – explains in *Fighters Over the Desert* by Christopher Shores and Hans Ring:

> The Hurricane was of course vastly superior to the CR 42 in speed and armament and also carried armour plating; this aircraft quickly gave us air supremacy. However, the manoeuvrability of the CR 42s in comparison to the Hurri-canes, made them difficult to shoot down once they had seen you unless they were foolish enough to endeavour to dis-engage by diving, and most of us fought many engagements with CR 42s which developed into an unending series of inconclusive, but very frightening, head-on attacks as the Italian fighters turned to meet us each time as we came in . . .
> [Unfortunately] our results against the Italians had been so good that perhaps we were a little over-confident and had not sufficiently absorbed the tactical lessons of the war in Europe. This all combined to give us a very rough time for the first few weeks after the Messerschmitts arrived.

This lack of experience of modern air combat meant that RAF fighters in North Africa frequently still flew in tight, complicated formations. These would indeed prove very vulnerable to the more flexible 109s. As late as 14 January 1942, 94 Squadron, when trying out a new formation for the first time, was attacked by just two 109s which shot down four Hurricanes – though only one pilot was killed – and badly damaged three more.

However, the greatest problem faced by the RAF, and indeed the Army, during the early part of the Desert War was the constant claims of other theatres. The campaigns in East Africa, while very satisfactory, provided one such distraction, though at least the Hurricanes of 1 Squadron SAAF did return from Eritrea in May 1941; on the 16th Captain Quirk won a DSO by landing behind enemy lines to rescue Lieutenant Burger who had force-landed – a trick which the Hurricane's strength and reliability enabled its pilots to repeat on several later occasions. Hurricanes were also among the ground and air forces which had to be diverted first against pro-Axis sympathizers in Iraq, then against the Vichy French in Syria, through which they had allowed the Germans to send weapons and aircraft to Iraq. Both these campaigns were necessary, both were successful, but both meant that valuable men and equipment were not available for the crucial fighting in Cyrenaica.

By far the most harmful of these diversions occurred during February and March 1941. It seemed at this time that almost every experienced Army or RAF unit was being sent to the aid of Greece, a country already at war with Italy and now threatened by a German invasion as well. Their departure was singularly ill-timed for it coincided with the arrival in North Africa of small but potent German ground and air forces under the command of a general named Erwin Rommel whom Hitler had personally selected to assist the hapless Italians.

Taking full advantage of his enemies' problems, on 31 March Rommel began a daring advance which re-conquered almost the whole of Cyrenaica, but he was unable to continue his progress into Egypt because there was one vital exception to his list of successes. The port of Tobruk, which he needed for his supplies and which threatened his lines of communication, still held out. This was due in no small measure to the resistance offered to his airmen and the attacks made on his columns by Hurricanes. Particular mention should be made of 73 Squadron and the Hurricane flight of No. 6 Squadron (which was equipped mainly with Lysanders). Both operated from landing strips within the defended perimeter around a besieged Tobruk in the fighter and army co-operation roles until 25 April and 8 May respectively. They suffered severely in the process but by the time that the few Hurricanes which remained flew out, the survival of Tobruk had been ensured.

Nothing unfortunately could ensure the survival of Greece. The first RAF fighter squadron to arrive there was No. 80, equipped with Gladiators, but on 7 February 1941 its B Flight, stationed at Paramythia, 30 miles south of Greece's border with Albania – another of Mussolini's pre-war conquests – received six Hurricanes. On 20 February these went into action for the first time and Flight Lieutenant Marmaduke Thomas St John Pattle destroyed a Fiat G 50 monoplane fighter, thereby gaining his first victory while flying the Hawker fighter – but not his last. 'Pat' Pattle, as he was called throughout the RAF, was a South African who had already gained distinction flying Gladiators in the Western Desert and Greece, but it was his exploits in Hurricanes which would make him the top-scoring RAF 'ace' with forty confirmed victories officially accepted – and many of his colleagues believed that even this fell well short of his true total.

80 Squadron was later joined by the Hurricanes of 33 Squadron and the Gladiators of 112 Squadron and through February and March all three saw almost constant action. On 28 February they enjoyed their greatest triumph, claiming the destruction of twenty-seven Italian aircraft. It seems probable that there were some exaggerated or duplicated claims and though the Greek Army later reported that every one had been confirmed on the ground, it would appear that once more the same aircraft were counted several times over. Even so it is difficult to accept the much reduced official Italian statement of losses. Pattle, for instance, having shot down two Fiat BR 20 bombers, had to return to Paramythia temporarily since oil from his victims had splattered over his windscreen, reducing his visibility to almost nil. On returning to the fight, he sighted three CR 42s. Christopher Shores, this time teamed with Brian Cull and assisted by Nicola Malizia, quotes his Combat Report in *Air War for Yugoslavia, Greece and Crete 1940–41*:

I got behind them and put a long burst into all three. One went down vertically at once, but in case it was a trick I followed him. He was in difficulties, that was most obvious, and when it looked as if he was going straight into the sea I decided to go and see what the other two were up to. As I climbed again I was most surprised to see two parachutes float down past me.

Pattle had thus certainly brought down two CR 42s and, being no boaster, claimed the third as only a 'probable', though he was convinced he had killed the pilot. The Italians do confirm the loss of two CR 42s but if their records are correct, eleven more claimed by other pilots were not even damaged. While there may well have been duplicated kills reported by the airmen and by Greek soldiers, such a discrepancy can surely not be explained by this factor alone. It is suggested therefore that the reason why the losses of biplane fighters were not mentioned is because they were not replaced, their units receiving more modern aircraft instead.

There is no argument that not a single Hurricane was lost. One Gladiator came down but the pilot baled out unhurt.

On 6 April the Germans finally intervened, invading both Yugoslavia and Greece. On the same day the RAF in Greece had its first clash with the Luftwaffe, the Hurricanes of 33 Squadron claiming to have destroyed five Messerschmitt Bf 109s without loss. The first two to go down – both incidentally confirmed in enemy records – fell victim to the extraordinary Pattle who had now been promoted to command 33 Squadron. Messrs Shores and Cull gave the following account of his successes as seen by another member of squadron, Pilot Officer 'Bill' Winsland:

This was my first really good look at a Hun from close quarters. I saw the C.O. beside me shoot down two of them in a few seconds. What a sight. I shall never forget it. What shooting too. A two-second burst from his eight guns at the first enemy machine caused a large piece to break off in mid-air, while the machine turned over vertically onto one wingtip as the pilot baled out – his parachute opened while his feet were still in the cockpit but he got clear in spite of the chute opening so soon. A similar fate awaited the second enemy machine which went spiralling down in flames. I did not have time to see what happened to its pilot.

As had happened in France, however, no amount of successes in the air could halt the enemy on the ground, and in any case the Hurricanes were soon struggling in the face of overwhelming odds. On 15 April, 33 Squadron's base at Larissa came under attack:

Flight Lieutenant Mackie, Pilot Officer Cheetham and Sergeant Genders were on dawn stand-by . . . Usually the stand-by Hurricanes simply warmed up their engines and then shut down. But this morning the engines continued to roar, and the three Hurricanes began to roll across the airfield. John Mackie had spotted fifteen Messerschmitt 109s coming in very low, obviously with the intention of strafing the airfield. The three Hurricanes had not yet left the ground when the 109s made their first pass, which was completed without a shot being fired. The German leader must have seen the trio taking off, and was deliberately letting them get into the air before he attacked. Three very brave pilots struggled with their controls to pull up the Hurricanes to a height which would give them a chance to make a fight of it, but their altimeters were barely registering 1,000 feet when the yellow-nosed Messerschmitts screamed down behind them with cannons blazing away.

Cheetham was the first to go . . . The onlookers, all standing in the open outside their ridge tents, such was the tension, saw Cheetham's Hurricane glide down, almost as if under control, and disappear behind some trees [the pilot being killed].

The Messerschmitt which had hit Cheetham now overshot the other two Hurricanes, and immediately John Mackie fastened on to its tail. He chased it right across the airfield. It was a fatal mistake. Another Messerschmitt came in close behind him. Mackie could have turned away and climbed out of trouble, as Sergeant Genders was now doing, but instead he deliberately hung on behind the 109 and opened fire. The pilot of the Messerschmitt baled out from 1,000 feet, while the plane belly-landed perfectly on its own in a field along-side the aerodrome, not far from the officers' mess tent . . .

In the meantime Mackie's Hurricane had been hit. It

93

staggered, went into a steepening dive, and finally flicked over the vertical in a most pathetic way, before hitting the ground and burning [Mackie also being killed].

Sergeant Genders had never taken part in a real dogfight before, but the youngster weaved and climbed away from the Messerschmitts like a veteran. He not only managed to escape with his life, but also shot down one of the Messerschmitts. He landed at Larissa when the yellow-noses had disappeared, without a bullet-hole in his aircraft.[2]

Thereafter matters rapidly went from bad to worse. On 20 April, a day of almost continuous combat saw the Hurricanes achieve many successes, but they also suffered their losses and among the dead was Squadron Leader Pattle who, though a sick man with a high temperature, had refused to withdraw from the fighting. Spotting a Hurricane in trouble with a Messerschmitt Bf 110 on its tail, Pattle unselfishly went to its aid though there were other enemy machines overhead which he must have known would pounce on him. He shot down the 110 in flames, but two others closed in from above, sending his Hurricane hurtling into the sea with a dead man slumped over the controls. On 23 April no less than thirteen Hurricanes were destroyed on the ground by an enemy raid. Next day the seven survivors took off for Crete, where further reinforcements joined them from time to time, though the number serviceable never rose above sixteen.

Since the Hurricanes on Crete also lacked the assistance of radar or proper ground control, and were so short of ammunition that they often went into action with six, sometimes only four, of their machine-guns loaded, they were scarcely in a position to deal effectively with the massive attacks which the Luftwaffe now delivered against the island in order to prepare the way for an airborne invasion. Individual achievements like those of the Australian, Flying Officer Vale, of 80 Squadron – who followed a distinguished career in Greece by claiming seven enemy aircraft over Crete – could not hope to affect the issue.

Equally, no amount of set-backs appear to have daunted the Hurricane pilots' resolve. A typical example of this occurred on 14 May. Squadron Leader Edward Howell, having arrived at Maleme airfield to take command of 33 Squadron, was being shown the layout of a Hurricane's cockpit – he had never previously flown the type – when events happened with startling rapidity. He describes them in his book *Escape to Live*:[3]

Suddenly there was the roar of engines starting up. I saw the other two Hurricanes take off in a cloud of dust . . . and prepared to start the engine. As soon as it kicked, I noticed the fitter pull the starter battery to one side and run; I thought 'this is efficiency – the boys run about their business!' Then I looked up. Through the subsiding dust, I saw the other two twisting and turning among a cloud of Me 109s. Even as I watched, an enemy aircraft dived into the ground in flames.

I opened the throttle and saw a string of five Messerschmitts coming in over the hill firing at me. It seemed an age before my wheels came off the strip. I went straight into a turn towards the approaching 109s, my wing tip within inches of the ground. My faithful old 'Hurrybus' took it without a murmur, the enemy flashed past and I went over instinctively into a steep turn the other way . . .

Enemy aircraft kept diving in on me in threes or fives. They were travelling fast and did not stay to fight. They just had a squirt at me and climbed away out of range again. It kept me fully occupied with evasive action. Out of the corner of my eye I saw two aircraft diving earthwards in flames. One was a Hurricane. There was no sign of the other . . .

Just level with me and about a mile away two 109s were turning in wide line astern formation. I headed in their direction . . . I drew in closer and closer with an eye on my own tail to make sure that I was not jumped. I restrained myself with difficulty. It is only the novice who opens at long range. I went right on the tail of the second 109 till I was in close formation on him. I could have lifted my nose and touched his tail with my prop . . . The Hurricane shook and shuddered as rounds poured into him, bits broke away and a white trail burst from his radiator as coolant came pouring out. He turned slowly to the right in a gentle dive. I was determined to see my first victory confirmed and made the mistake of following him down.[4] I had no difficulty as he was past taking evasive action and I continued pouring ammunition into him till I noticed tracer coming past me. The other 109 was on my tail. I realized my mistake and pulled quickly up into a turn to port, then flick rolled over into a steep turn the other way and found myself coming in on the enemy's quarter and gave him a burst . . . He was certainly full of holes.

Yet for all their pilots' bravery, by 19 May only four Hurricanes remained fit for action. These were ordered back to Egypt, and although later attempts were made to fly in reinforcements and Hurricanes with long-range fuel tanks carried out necessarily brief sorties over the island, Crete thereafter had no real fighter protection. After a violent struggle it fell to German airborne troops, its British and Commonwealth defenders suffering heavy casualties – as indeed did the Royal Navy from constant air attacks. Nonetheless their resistance was certainly not wasted. For German losses of more than 6,000 men resulted in them never daring to risk a similar airborne operation, even against a target of far greater strategic value – Malta.

NOTES

1 In practice before the flights started their dangers were slightly reduced by French Equatorial Africa becoming no longer hostile, having accepted the leadership of General de Gaulle.

2 E.C.R. Baker: *Pattle: Supreme Fighter in the Air*. His account of this episode is based on the recollections of an eyewitness, Flying Officer George Rumsey, 33 Squadron's Adjutant. Enemy records confirm that Sergeant Genders as well as Flight Lieutenant Mackie did destroy a Bf 109.

3 Howell was captured when Crete fell – hence the book's title.

4 Enemy records reveal that Howell's belief was correct. He had indeed achieved his first confirmed victory.

Chapter 8

Island under Siege

The Hurricane was on Malta too. Everyone has heard how the island-fortress was defended by three Sea Gladiators called 'Faith, Hope and Charity' – although in reality there were about half a dozen Gladiators on hand, if probably never more than three airborne at any one time – but few realize how brief was the period when they provided the sole fighter protection. Mussolini declared war on Britain and France on 10 June 1940; on 28 June the first four Hurricanes led by Flight Lieutenant 'Jock' Barber reached Malta from North Africa.

No further reinforcements arrived for over a month, but though the Italians, who could muster about 200 machines in Sicily, a mere 60 miles distant, made daily air raids, this handful of fighters mounted a sturdy resistance. They not only took their toll of their attackers but for a time they enjoyed an almost miraculous immunity – so much so that it was a profound shock to servicemen and civilians alike when, on 16 July, Flight Lieutenant Keeble became the first pilot to die in Malta's defence. One witness of this sad event was Wing Commander – later Air Commodore – Carter Jonas who was the Station Commander at Luqa airfield. In *Malta: The Hurricane Years 1940–41* by Christopher Shores and Brian Cull with Nicola Malizia, he gives this simple but moving account:

The sounds of firing and diving aircraft had almost ceased when Peter Keeble was killed, his Hurricane rocketing down out of a patch of blue sky, flattening out for a moment as if to attempt some sort of landing, and then diving into the ground to the right of the wireless masts at Rinella . . . A day or two later we buried him in the quiet little cemetery up at Bighi, with the wind sighing in the fir trees overhead.

On 2 August the long-awaited reinforcements were at last received when twelve Hurricanes of 418 Flight, guided by two Fleet Air Arm Skuas, took off from the carrier *Argus*, then south of Sardinia, and headed for Malta. All reached the island safely, where they amalgamated with Malta's existing fighter flight to form 261 Squadron under Squadron Leader Balden. Their arrival was slightly marred by an over-exuberant display by Sergeant 'Fred' Robertson. 'Jock' Barber – who would later attain the rank of Group Captain – describes what happened in *Malta: The Hurricane Years 1940–41*:

> Sgt Robertson and two [other] Sergeant Pilots arrived in a vic formation over Luqa – very, very low and fast beat-up of the airfield, then a roll off the top. Robertson made a typical Naval 'split-arse' approach and as he made the final turn his motor cut. The aircraft turned upside down and went through three stone walls. However he only sustained minor concussion and was flying again within a few days.

Robertson like many other pilots had cause to be grateful for the strength of his Hurricane. As indeed had the people of Malta for by the time he left the island in April 1941, he had become one of 261 Squadron's most successful airmen, his 'kills' including a Savoia Marchetti SM 79 shot down at night on 18 December 1940.

The importance of this *Argus* mission, which with nice double meaning was code-named Operation HURRY, may be judged from the fact that the little carrier was guarded by her much larger sister HMS *Ark Royal*, the battleships *Valiant* and *Resolution*, the cruisers *Enterprise* and *Arethusa* and ten destroyers. This in turn reflected the growing realization on both sides that Malta was the key to success or failure in the campaigns in North Africa: 'the rock', in the words of the Italian Official History, 'upon which our hopes in the Mediterranean foundered'.

Malta's task was to be a permanent threat to the Axis supply routes to North Africa. Whereas the Allies had to provision their armies by means of vessels travelling more than 14,000 miles round the Cape of Good Hope, their enemies had only a few hundred miles of the central Mediterranean to cross. It might have seemed certain therefore that the Axis strength would quickly be built up to a level far exceeding anything that the British could match. Instead the reverse proved the case and the reason was that forces operating from Malta not only crippled all Axis movements but decimated the Italian merchant marine.

At first Malta's main contribution to the Allied cause was the reconnaissance work carried out by her Glenn Martin Marylands – this was sufficiently valuable to earn the personal thanks of Admiral Cunningham. The island, however, would soon provide a base for Wellington bombers and Swordfish torpedo-planes, while early in 1941 submarines would join them in preying on the Axis supply lines, as would Royal Navy destroyers in April.

This build-up of Malta's striking power coincided with and was made possible by a build-up of her fighter defences. In view of what has been said it may at first seem surprising that no further attempt was made to fly off Hurricanes to Malta until 17 November, but of course on 8 August the Battle of Britain had commenced at full intensity and every Hurricane was needed at home. Unhappily, when the supply of fighters to Malta was resumed with Operation WHITE the results were very different from those attending Operation HURRY.

Once again twelve Hurricanes and two Skuas took off successfully from *Argus*, but this time they had further to fly. Vice Admiral Somerville who commanded the escorting Force H had been faced with a difficult decision. It is described in his Official Report, in turn recorded by Ian Cameron in *Red Duster, White Ensign:The story of the Malta Convoys*:

It seemed to me
1.The Italians were probably aware of our departure from Gibraltar.

2. They might well consider engaging Force H with their superior forces . . .

In view of this I deemed it advisable to fly off the Hurricanes from a position as far to the west as weather would permit. In reply to an enquiry, *Argus* informed me that with the wind as at present the Hurricanes could be flown off from [a point forty miles to the west of that previously agreed upon].

Unfortunately the wind did not remain 'as at present'. Instead it veered round to blow almost directly against the aircraft, the pilots of which moreover had been briefed to fly not at the Hurricane's best altitude of 10,000 feet but at 2,000, where in the 'heavier' lower air their range was much diminished. When the first section of one Skua leading six Hurricanes made a rendezvous with a Sunderland flying-boat from Malta, it was already 25 minutes behind schedule. On the final stage of the journey two Hurricanes ran out of fuel and were forced to 'ditch'. The Sunderland was able to rescue one pilot but the other was lost.

The observer in the Skua guiding the second section was on his first flight out of training school. The weather was now rapidly worsening, bringing patches of thick sea mist. In the increasingly difficult conditions this section failed to meet up with its Sunderland. The Skua finally made a landfall in Sicily, where it was promptly shot down by AA fire. The Hurricanes were never seen again.

Thus only four Hurricanes were added to the strength of 261 Squadron and it would not increase its numbers further until January 1941 when twelve Hurricanes arrived in crates and six more flew in from newly captured bases in Cyrenaica. Nonetheless by the end of November 1940 Malta's fighters had been credited with thirty-seven successes and the Regia Aeronautica, which had originally made unescorted bombing raids, had felt compelled to provide strong fighter protection, eventually appearing mainly after dark.

261 Squadron could well be proud of its achievements for the Italians enjoyed many advantages apart from sheer weight of numbers, not least the fact that the calibre of their airmen seems

to have been higher than in North Africa or Greece. In *Malta: The Hurricane Years*, Messrs Shores and Cull quote Sergeant – later Flight Lieutenant – Pickering, one of the pilots to reach the island in August 1940, as confirming that:

> The quality of Italian pilots was very good. The CR 42s came between the Gladiators and Hurricanes in performance, but their pilots were aggressive and skilled. A stern attack by a Hurricane on a CR 42 could result in the CR 42 pulling upwards sharply and at the top of a loop, opening head-on at the Hurricane while he was inverted. It was necessary for the Hurricanes to use air tactics for attacking CR 42s similar to those used by Bf 109s against Hurricanes.
>
> The original Macchis [C 200s] were faster than the CR 42s but less manoeuvrable. Their tactical handling was not good and one suspects that they were brought into service with insufficient practice combat experience. The S 79 bombers were operationally obsolete . . . One can only admire the courage of pilots who flew it on offensive missions, because almost any hit could bring it down – usually in flames . . .
>
> . . . S 79 raids were made at between 15,000 feet and 18,000 feet (I think). There was insufficient [radar] warning for Hurricanes to climb to 20,000 feet before raiders were over the target . . . If one climbed up below a raid, the fighter escort of the raiders could pounce on the climbing Hurricanes when they were most vulnerable and un-manoeuvrable. If the Hurricanes climbed towards Sicily to intercept raiders on their return flight, they would be bounced by the second fighter escort (the relative speeds of CR 42s and S 79s and the range of CR 42s required this return flight 'back-up').
>
> The main tactic became for Hurricanes to gain height in a climb to the South of the Island and then turn North to try and get to 20,000 feet over the raiders after they had turned for home. This would have been more effective with better radar, but vectoring and height information was not very accurate.

The defenders' difficulties were about to increase dramatically. Among 261 Squadron's victims had been at least two Junkers Ju 87 Stuka dive-bombers manned by Italian crews. In January 1941 Stukas and Junkers Ju 88s manned by members of the Luftwaffe reached Sicily. On the 10th they inflicted massive damage on the aircraft carrier *Illustrious*. She managed to limp to Malta but it was clear that the enemy would attempt to finish her off before she could effect the temporary repairs needed to take her to safety.

On 16 January the expected assault was made by about eighty German bombers. Difficulties in keeping the Hurricanes service-able – they frequently had to use parts from other types of damaged aircraft – meant that the enemy could only be engaged by half a dozen of them, plus three Fulmars from *Illustrious*. Yet so determined were the efforts of the pilots, supported by a very well-directed anti-aircraft barrage, that the Germans made just one bomb hit on the carrier which caused only minor damage – though unfortunately those bombs that missed their target did result in heavy civilian casualties in neighbouring residential areas.

It was undoubtedly a tribute to the disruption the fighters had caused that when the Luftwaffe returned on 18 January it attacked not the carrier but two of Malta's airfields, Luqa and Hal Far: the third, Takali, was already inoperative after heavy rain. They put Luqa out of action for a time, but when they resumed their attempts to destroy *Illustrious* next day, the Hurricanes were still able to intervene effectively. Only slight damage was inflicted by near misses, there were few civilian casualties this time and the enemy mounted no further assaults before 23 January, on the night of which *Illustrious* slipped out of Grand Harbour, to reach Alexandria, battered but intact, two days later.

Not that her departure ended the Luftwaffe's attacks on Malta. Its bombers concentrated on the airfields, while Messerschmitt Bf 109s, which were superior to 261 Squadron's old Hurricane Is at higher altitudes, attacked them from above as they climbed to engage. As the weeks passed without respite and casualties mounted, the exhaustion of the squadron's pilots grew and it appears that their morale inevitably declined. Nonetheless they stuck grimly to their task and they still continued to shoot down enemy bombers – as witness this vivid account by South African Flying Officer Charles Laubscher, recorded in *Malta: The Hurricane Years*:

I was leading Sgt Peter Jordan on a patrol when we were vectored onto a flight of Ju 87s which had attacked the Grand Harbour. They had turned back to Sicily and I couldn't see a formation but spotted a straggler who, curiously enough, was flying diagonally across our line of approach and not heading pell-mell for home. He was only 100 or so feet above the sea and we closed on him rapidly. I instructed Peter to keep a sharp look out for enemy fighters and then to follow me. I started a quarter stern attack and had the unpleasant experience of flying down the middle of a cone of tracer from the rear gunner. I held my fire until the enemy was within range. When I pressed the button there was the ripping noise that was characteristic of the Hurricane's eight guns and I saw strikes on the fuselage of the Stuka. The rear gunner was killed by that burst, as his gun swung up to a vertical position as he slumped down. I tried to turn in behind him but found that I was going to overshoot and pulled away to starboard. I swung in a wide circle around the machine climbing slightly to lose speed and came in at him again from dead ahead and slightly above. The pilot of the Stuka had plenty of courage and pulled up his nose to have a crack at me with his forward firing guns. I was so surprised that I involuntarily pulled up slightly and I passed over him before I could get him in my gunsight again. At that moment Peter came in from the port quarter, misjudged his deflection by a fraction and blew off the Stuka's tail. When I turned I saw a long patch of the fluorescent dye that the Germans carried staining the sea a light yellow-green but could not pick out the pilot. Nevertheless we circled the spot and radioed Control to get a radar fix on us and send out a crash boat. They never found him and I often wondered whether he went in with his machine and dead gunner or whether he managed to bale out and was picked up by the flyingboat they had stationed in Sicily for sea rescue work.

103

This incident occurred as late as 9 May but by that time in any case the situation in Malta was starting to improve. In early April twelve Hurricane IIAs took off from *Ark Royal*. The lessons of Operation WHITE had been learned and all reached Malta, where with their improved rate of climb they could meet the enemy more effectively. On 27 April twenty-three more Hurricanes arrived, having again flown off *Ark Royal*, and on 12 May the new recruits were formed into 185 Squadron. On 21 May the Hurricanes of 249 Squadron were also ferried to the island – appearing in the middle of an air raid! This increase in strength allowed 261 Squadron to retire to the Middle East, much to the relief of pilots who were now well overdue for a long period of rest.

The raid which had greeted 249 Squadron had been made by the Regia Aeronautica as the Luftwaffe was now retiring from Sicily to participate in the fighting in the Balkans. Full advantage was taken of this relaxation of pressure, for during June there was a steady series of operations, ferrying Hurricane IIs to Malta. Among these were Malta's first cannon-armed Mark IICs, some of which went to 185 Squadron while others provided the equipment for a new unit, 126 Squadron. Still more Hurricanes arrived in September, while on 12 November the Hurricane IIBs of 242 and 605 Squadrons left *Argus* and *Ark Royal* for Malta – the last service the noble *Ark* would render, for she was sunk by a U-boat when returning to Gibraltar. In practice, however, all these latest arrivals were incorporated into 126 or 249 Squadrons.

Thus throughout the second half of 1941 there were three Hurricane squadrons defending Malta by day, while smaller Hurricane units were entrusted with night-fighter or reconnaissance duties. Furthermore the day-fighter squadrons carried out a number of tasks apart from the interception of enemy raiders, particularly on the night of 25–26 July when the Italians delivered a seaborne assault on a convoy at anchor in Grand Harbour. The attackers numbered eight one-man explosive motorboats supported by two larger MAS-boats – the initials stood for 'Motoscafo Armato Silurante', Italian for Motor Torpedo boat. Their fate is described by Sergeant Zammitt of the

Royal Malta Artillery who was on duty at Fort St Elmo and whose recollections appear in *Faith Hope and Charity* by Kenneth Poolman:[1]

Suddenly I heard the sound of an MTB and although it was still twilight I saw a small MTB three hundred yards away heading towards the breakwater bridge. I gave the alarm and my gun went into action just as the MTB hit the bridge and blew up. Searchlights illuminated the scene. A hundred yards away from the bridge I saw another small craft. I directed the gun onto it and with the first two shots hit it and blew it up. I again directed the gun onto a third one a hundred yards away and with the first few rounds it was destroyed. I saw three others heading towards Grand Harbour. All guns fired at them. One was destroyed and two disabled. About a quarter of an hour later I saw two small suspicious objects at about 2,000 yards away . . . They were sunk . . .

Just after all this I saw two large MTBs [the MAS-boats] far away and out of range of my gun. These were being engaged by the Hurricanes.

They were indeed. Flight Lieutenant Lefevre of 126 Squadron, a native of the Channel Islands, attacked a MAS-boat so repeatedly that the crew hoisted a white flag. Both enemy vessels were crippled, one later sinking. A Hurricane of 185 squadron was also lost but Pilot Officer Winton baled out and took to his rubber dinghy. His subsequent experiences are related with deceptive lightheartedness in the Squadron Diary:

For the next few hours he sunbathed, played with a friendly turtle, wondered who would have his motor-cycle, and then spotted a stationary torpedo-boat. He paddled the dinghy with his hands and, finding progress slow, towed it and swam towards the boat. By climbing up the side he was able to peer into it and was confronted by eight very much dead Italians.

Taking possession of the boat was thus quite easy and as he couldn't start it, he waited . . . [Six hours after he had baled out] a Swordfish with floats dropped in to pay him a visit and

105

gave him and the [Italian naval] flag, a lift home, where he again took possession of his motor-cycle.[2]

Even before this, Hurricanes had been engaging Italian targets other than those encountered in the air and indeed seeking them out over Italy's own territory. In *The Hawker Hurricane*, Francis K. Mason quotes another extract from 185 Squadron's Diary, this time in early July:

> Four Hurricanes (S/L Mould, S/L Rabagliati, F/L Jefferies and Sgt Mackay) took off to straf the seaplane base at Syracuse . . . Having between them destroyed six flying-boats, damaged four others and severely shaken everyone in the neighbourhood of Syracuse, S/L Mould broke the world's low flying record (four inches above the sea) from Syracuse back to Malta.[3]

Other similar missions by Hurricanes followed, and they also escorted Blenheims when these raided targets in Sicily. Such attacks were, however, the smallest part of the offensive that Malta was now delivering as her bombers, submarines and surface vessels all concentrated on Italy's luckless merchant ships, quite regardless of their own losses.

In September 28 per cent of all supplies sent to Rommel in North Africa failed to reach him; in October the proportion lost was 21 per cent. In November it rose to a staggering 63 per cent, just at the time when the Allies were commencing a major operation. It must therefore be a matter for wonder that General Sir Claude Auchinleck who, having succeeded Wavell as C-in-C, Middle East, was the chief beneficiary of Malta's efforts, showed neither appreciation of nor gratitude for them; he even stated that the retention of the island was not absolutely necessary for his plans. It was as well that the Navy and Air Force Commanders, with the full support of Churchill, had greater strategic insight.

Unfortunately, so had Hitler. He had come to realize that the Axis cause in North Africa suffered when Malta was strong, whereas when Malta was weak, it prospered. Diverting large aerial forces from Russia, he ordered their commander, Field Marshal

Kesselring, to 'ensure safe lines of communication' to Rommel by bringing about the 'suppression' of the island-fortress.

Kesselring certainly did his level best and the first four months of 1942 saw Malta reeling under an ever-increasing weight of bombs. On 7 March fifteen Spitfires flew in from the carrier *Eagle*, to be followed by others later that same month. They were the first such fighters to operate outside the British Isles – a measure this of the unsupported burden the Hurricanes had carried for so long – and they now re-equipped 126 and 249 Squadrons. With their faster speed and rate of climb the Spitfires found it easier to tackle the German raiders, but being less robust than the Hurricanes they were also put out of action more easily. Even when the Americans generously made available the fleet carrier USS *Wasp*, from which on 20 April forty-seven Spitfires took off for Malta, the vast majority were quickly rendered unserviceable, mainly by attacks on their own airfields.

It was thus the Hurricane pilots who continued to uphold Malta's cause in the face of growing German air superiority. The raids in March doubled those in February, and those in April all but doubled the raids in March. On 27 March 229 Squadron with ten Hurricane IICs left North Africa for Malta, where its personnel took over additional aircraft that had previously belonged to 126 or 249 Squadrons. Hurricanes also still equipped 185 Squadron, four members of which gained one of the most remarkable victories of the campaign on 21 March when defending the airfield at Hal Far. Sergeant – later Squadron Leader – Ray Hesselyn of 249 Squadron was visiting the base at the time, and in *Malta: The Spitfire Year 1942*[4] by Christopher Shores and Brian Cull with Nicola Malizia, appears an unusual eyewitness account of Hurricane pilots in action – by a Spitfire 'ace' watching from the ground:

Eight Me 110s came out of the sun in a shallow dive . . . but all the bombs fell short and none hit the aerodrome. The Me 110s machine-gunned the aerodrome as they passed over . . . [I] saw four Hurricanes diving out of the sun onto the tails of the bombers, which were straggled out line abreast. The Hurricanes opened fire as the bombers crossed the coast, apparently taking the 110s by surprise. It was point blank range, and almost simultaneously four of the 110s dived seawards. Two of them burst into flames, flicked over and fell straight into the drink. The other two lazily rolled on their backs and then dropped straight into the sea. The remaining four 110s at once broke, and began weaving, each steering a different course for home. Splitting up, the Hurricanes gave chase to the 110s, shooting down two more before returning to base.

It is not clear whether Hesselyn personally saw the last two 110s go down or whether he was merely repeating the accounts given by 185 Squadron's pilots later. It is quite certain, however, that an experienced, independent eyewitness could confirm the destruction of four enemy aircraft beyond doubt. That only one such loss is recorded in enemy records might therefore come as a surprise – except that by now it must have become obvious that these are far from complete. It may be noted incidentally that no 110 was ever again seen over Malta during the hours of daylight.

But far more important than any individual successes was the fact that the defenders kept up their resistance for just long enough. Kesselring had advised Hitler that Malta had been neutralized – with some justification since by now he had forced her bombers and submarines to leave the island – but in any event the Führer had no real choice. He had to transfer aircraft to Russia and North Africa, from both of which the demands for them had become too great to be resisted. The German attacks did not cease, but from the end of April they no longer continued at their former murderous intensity.

It was just the opportunity Malta needed to restore her shattered defences. On 9 May *Wasp* was back with forty-seven more Spitfires; HMS *Eagle* added seventeen more. And this time the Luftwaffe did not destroy them on the ground. By the beginning of June 229 Squadron had left the island and 185 Squadron had converted to Spitfires, as did 1435 Flight, the Hurricane night-fighter unit, in July.

Yet the Hurricane's most important contribution to Malta's survival still lay in the future. Like any besieged fortress, the island could resist only as long as it possessed certain essential commodities. Foremost of course was food. Next came oil which provided Malta's power for everything from flour mills and water pumps to the cranes in Grand Harbour; kerosene which on a treeless island supplied the means for all light and heat; and war materials such as aviation fuel and ammunition.

Malta could only keep up her stocks of these if convoys reached her safely. It was therefore a source of terrible anxiety that of late they had not done so. The Axis airmen had struck not only at Malta but at her supply routes, and in January 1942 a victory in Cyrenaica had given them new airfields from which vessels coming from Alexandria could be attacked, while at the same time depriving the RAF of the bases from which they could be given fighter protection. It was not for nothing that the seas between Crete and Cyrenaica became known thereafter as 'Bomb Alley'.

In February three merchantmen making for Malta from Alexandria came under such heavy air attack that two were sunk and the third had to turn back, badly damaged. No provisions reached the island. In March another convoy was mauled by the Luftwaffe. Only two ships reached Grand Harbour and they were later sunk at their moorings after less than one-fifth of their supplies had been unloaded.

By June the situation was desperate. The rations issued to troops and civilians alike, already severely limited, were cut to the absolute minimum and unpleasant skin diseases caused by malnutrition had begun to appear. Every drop of oil had to be guarded jealously; the Governor, Viscount Gort, set a necessary example by using a bicycle as his mode of transport. Unless Malta could make good her deficiencies quickly she would soon exhaust her last reserves and be left with no choice but to surrender.

That this did not occur owed much to the pilots of another version of the Hawker Hurricane.

NOTES

1 This is a singularly misleading title since the book covers the air defence of Malta for the whole period of the siege, though it does give a particularly detailed account of the exploits of Malta's Gladiators.

2 Quoted in *The Air Battle of Malta: The Official Account of the RAF*

in Malta June 1940 to November 1942, prepared for the Air Ministry by the Ministry of Information. Winton kept the Italian ensign as a souvenir for his squadron.

3 We have met Squadron Leader Mould before, when as a young pilot officer with No. 1 Squadron he shot down the first enemy aircraft to be destroyed by a Hurricane in France. He was killed in action on 1 October 1941.

4 Though it is worth a reminder that Spitfires did not reach Malta at all until March 1942 or take over the main fighter defence until May.

Chapter 9

The Convoys Went Through

As early as the Norwegian campaign Hurricanes had taken off from an aircraft carrier without any trouble and had even landed back on it with the aid of unofficial improvisations. It was natural therefore that the Royal Navy should feel that Hurricanes could well be adapted so as to serve on board carriers. In the early summer of 1941 the adaptations were made and thereafter the Sea Hurricane claimed a place in the Hurricane's overall history – albeit a somewhat confusing one.

No exact record of Sea Hurricane numbers exists because they were not new machines leaving the production lines, but existing ones converted for a new purpose; it was probably between 500 and 550. Confusingly also, the first carrier-based aircraft were called Sea Hurricane IBs – we will come to the IAs later. The early IBs were ex-RAF Mark Is, with Merlin III engines – which from 1942 were boosted so as to increase their speed to about 315 mph – eight machine guns and such useful additions as an arrester hook below the fuselage which would catch the crosswires on a carrier's deck. Subsequently, however, the Fleet Air Arm flew Sea Hurricanes which had more modern engines and sometimes up to twelve machine guns, but were still frequently known as Sea Hurricane IBs, though they were also called 'Hooked Hurricane IIs'.

Then came the Sea Hurricane IC which originally had a Mark I fuselage and a Merlin III engine, but had been fitted with the four-cannon wings carried on the Mark IIC, as well as the necessary adaptations for use on carriers. Some Hawker histories refer to large totals of these being produced, while other accounts suggest that they were few in number, as do Admiralty records. This latter view may gain support from the fact that such machines must have had only a very limited performance.

The reason for the apparent discrepancy may have been that, just as the designation Sea Hurricane IB included aircraft that were not in reality Hurricane Is, some references to Sea Hurricane ICs included aeroplanes that should really have been described as Sea Hurricane IICs. It appears that some Mark Is were converted not only by the addition of the four-cannon wing but by being re-engined with later models of the Merlin as well. It is certain that in late 1942 the Fleet Air Arm obtained thirty sets of IIC wings which were fitted to existing Sea Hurricanes with Mark II engines but hitherto armed only with machine guns. And in early 1943 about sixty RAF IICs were converted to carry full Fleet Air Arm equipment. These were the finest of the Sea Hurricanes. Their Merlin XXs gave them a top speed of 318 mph, they had a service ceiling of 34,500 feet and they could climb to 20,000 feet in nine minutes.

But whatever their correct designations or their precise details, the Royal Navy Hurricanes possessed all the sturdy reliability of their RAF sisters. They flew from a total of six fleet carriers and seven escort carriers. They made their first 'kill' on 31 July 1941, when Lieutenant Commander Judd and Sub-Lieutenant Howarth of 880 Squadron, serving on carrier *Furious* in Arctic waters, destroyed a Dornier Do 18 flying-boat. They made their last as late as 26 May 1944, when 835 Squadron from HMS *Nairana* downed two four-engined Junkers Ju 290s over the Bay of Biscay; and they were still covering Arctic convoys three months after that.

Sea Hurricanes operated in the Indian Ocean as well as the Arctic and Atlantic. In May 1942 they protected Allied landings at Diego Suarez in Vichy French Madagascar which led to the occupation of the whole of that island. This, however, was little more than a practice for their part in a much more important assault on Vichy French territory in November 1942: the invasion of Algeria, to which Churchill had given the inspiring name of Operation TORCH.

Nor was this the Sea Hurricanes' most vital contribution to the war in the Mediterranean. That had been made earlier in their protection of two crucial convoys to Malta. The first of these, code-named HARPOON, passed through the Straits of Gibraltar on 12 June 1942. At the same time another convoy, code-named VIGOROUS, left Alexandria for Malta. Both came under relentless air attack, and the convoy from Alexandria, which lacked fighter cover, was compelled to turn back on 15 June.

By contrast the six merchantmen in HARPOON were guarded by the carriers *Eagle* and *Argus*, the latter's fighters being Fulmars, while the former was equipped with twelve Sea Hurricanes of 801 Squadron and four Sea Hurricanes of 813 Squadron, as well as four Fulmars. It should be noted that the carriers were not intended to accompany the convoy all the way to Malta, but only as far as the Narrows – the waters between Sicily and Tunisia – where they would turn back. The merchantmen would pass through the Narrows at night, then make their final dash for Malta. It was appreciated that losses would occur on this last stage but it was hoped that the Fleet Air Arm fighters would give the convoy a sufficiently 'good start' to allow the bulk of the supplies to get through.

The 'good start' was certainly achieved. On 14 June almost 150 German and Italian dive-bombers, high-level bombers and torpedo-planes from Sardinia and Sicily, escorted by over 100 fighters, made a series of attacks. They found the handful of naval fighters more than ready to receive them:

I finished the entire 12 seconds of ammunition and must have been closer than 100 yards at the end. I saw the de Wilde ammunition hitting his port wing, sparkling like firecrackers. Bits of the aircraft flew past me. Or so it seemed – or they might have been the rear gunner's empty shell cases. I was sure I had hit him and mortally wounded him. I saw a burst of smoke from his port wing root again, this time after I had finished firing all my ammunition . . . The Ju 88 flew on in a shallow dive and I found myself easily overtaking him. He had slowed right down to about 160 knots. I was sure he was a 'goner'.

113

Sub-Lieutenant Michael Crosley of 813 Squadron, whose account is quoted in *Malta: The Spitfire Year* had indeed shot down his target which was only one of ten enemy aircraft destroyed by the Sea Hurricanes on the 14th – and they 'bagged' two more during the course of the operation. The Fulmars downed another four and the AA gunners several others. Three Sea Hurricanes and four Fulmars also fell but so effective were their interceptions that only one merchantman was lost before the carriers turned back to Gibraltar. Deprived of their guardians, three more of the convoy, including a precious tanker, were sunk next day, but in the early hours of the 16th the two survivors reached Malta, their 15,000 tons of food and ammunition providing at least a breathing space for the battered island-fortress.

It was obvious to everyone, however, that Malta's fate had merely been postponed. Another bigger convoy was detailed to sail in August – from Gibraltar so that carrier-based fighters could guard it for at least part of its journey. It was even considered sending the heavy fleet units all the way to Malta. The suggestion was eventually rejected but not without considerable anguish for it was realized that if this convoy – code-named PEDESTAL – did not get through there would be no time to mount another one before the island's remaining stocks of food, oil and kerosene ran out completely.

Malta's lifeline consisted of thirteen big, fast freighters, two of them American, packed with a mixture of food, ammunition and aviation fuel in cans, plus the tanker *Ohio*. She too had been supplied by the generous Americans since no British tanker could make the speed necessary to keep up with the convoy, but she was manned by a hand-picked British crew under Captain Dudley Mason. To escort these vessels Vice-Admiral Syfret, the South African officer who had succeeded Somerville in command of 'Force H', was given the battleships *Nelson* and *Rodney*, seven cruisers, twenty-six destroyers and, best of all, three aircraft-carriers to provide the convoy with its 'good start'.

The three carriers were *Victorious* equipped mainly with Fulmars, but also with five Sea Hurricanes of 885 Squadron, *Indomitable* embarking twenty-two Sea Hurricanes of 800 and 880 Squadrons as well as Grumman Martlets, the Fleet Air Arm version of the US Navy's Wildcat, and *Eagle* on which were sixteen Sea Hurricanes of 801 and 813 Squadrons, together with four more as reserves. This was an impressive strength by the Royal Navy's standards of the time but entirely justified by the issues at stake. Unfortunately the Axis were equally aware of these and had gathered some 500 aircraft in Sardinia and Sicily with instructions to prevent the merchantmen from reaching Malta at all costs.

Nor was air attack the only threat to PEDESTAL. In the afternoon of 11 August a U-boat torpedoed *Eagle* just after four Sea Hurricanes of 801 Squadron had taken off. One of these was flown by Sub-Lieutenant – later Lieutenant Commander – Peter Hutton, who relates in Brian Johnson's *Fly Navy: The History of Marine Aviation* that:

> I remember clearly looking round to see the ship beginning to list. I was able to see aircraft still on deck slither off over the side and I realized I was not going to land back on her.[1]

Just before sunset the Luftwaffe mounted its first major raid. Sub-Lieutenant Hugh Popham of 880 Squadron was one of the pilots who engaged this and he describes what happened in his book *Sea Flight*:

> The Tannoy crackled. 'Scramble the Hurricanes. Scramble the Hurricanes!'
> The fitters in the cockpits pressed the starter-buttons and the four Merlins opened up with a blast of sound and a gust of blue smoke. As we scrambled up the wings, the crews hopped out the other side, fixing our straps with urgent fingers. Connect RT; switch on ten degrees of flap. Trim. Quick cockpit check. The ship was under full helm, racing up into wind – and we were off and climbing at full boost on a northerly vector to 20,000 feet, head swivelling. Down to 12,000; alter course; climb to 20,000 again. And there they were, a big formation of 88s below us. One after another we peeled off and went down after them. They broke formation as they saw us coming and [Lieutenant] Brian [Fiddes] and I picked one and went after him. He turned and dived away,

and we stuffed the nose down, full bore, willing our aircraft to make up on him. At extreme range we gave him a long burst; bits came off and smoke poured out of one engine, and then he vanished into the thickening twilight . . . We re-formed . . . and started to climb back to base.

The sight we saw took our breath away. The light was slowly dying, and the ships were no more than a pattern on the grey steel plate of the sea; but where we had left them sailing peacefully through the sunset, now they were enclosed in a sparkling net of tracer and bursting shells, a mesh of fire. Every gun in the fleet and convoy was firing, and the darkling air was laced with threads and beads of fire.

. . . The light was going and we were running short of petrol . . . [and] they were firing at anything that flew . . . [but eventually when all but out of fuel] I . . . just managed to make out what looked like a carrier astern of the convoy . . . I could see by the wake that she was under helm . . . [but] there was a slight chance I might get down in one piece, even with the deck swinging: there was no chance of my getting round again. I continued my approach.

. . . Now I could see the deck, swerving away to starboard under me. It was my last chance. I crammed the nose down, cut the throttle, and with the last bit of extra speed, tried to kick the aircraft into a turn to match the ship's. She was swinging too fast. The wheels touched, and the skid wiped off the undercarriage and the aircraft hit the deck and [went] slithering and screeching up towards the island on its belly. I hung on and waited. It stopped at last, just short of the island, on the centre-line – what was left of it.

For a fraction of a second I was too relieved to move. And then, out of the corner of my eye, I saw a tongue of blue flame flicker across the bottom of the cockpit, and I yanked the pin out of the straps and was over the side. An instant later the wreck went up in a haze of flame.

It seemed excessively ignorant to have to ask which ship I was in;[2] and so I waited in the doorway into the island while the firecrews doused the blaze, and Jumbo the crane lurched up and removed the bits.

The air attack just recounted would prove little more than a reconnaissance in force for the massive assaults which came in at intervals throughout 12 August. All met resolute opposition from the defending fighters. Of these eight, including four Sea Hurricanes, were lost in combat, but it was reckoned that they had brought down between thirty-five and forty enemy aircraft, of which the Sea Hurricanes had claimed almost three-quarters. Lieutenant Cork of 880, whom we have met earlier when he served with Bader's 242 Squadron during the Battle of Britain, was credited with the destruction of five Axis warplanes on this day alone, a feat which earned him a DSO.

Despite a number of exaggerated or duplicated claims, there is no doubt that the Fleet Air Arm in general and the Sea Hurricanes in particular had done all that could have been asked of them. Time and again they had prevented the enemy from inflicting damage. The very first raid of the day for example had been so harried by Sea Hurricanes that only four of the attacking Junkers Ju 88s were able even to get past the fighters to bomb the convoy, and that ineffectively.

Far more effective was the last attack made before the carriers turned back. This was directed mainly against *Indomitable*, which was hit by two bombs and badly damaged. Her fighters were compelled to land on *Victorious* where several battle-scarred machines had to be pushed into the sea to gain the space needed on badly over-crowded decks. The Stukas responsible did not escape unhurt either, as demonstrated by the report of Sub-Lieutenant Blyth Ritchie of 800 Squadron which appears in *Malta: The Spitfire Year*:

I saw one Ju 87 at 400 feet and chased it for one mile approximately. I did a beam attack at 100 yards and saw part of the cowling fly off, then carried round to astern and closed to 60 yards and saw the gunner double up. It was now smoking and on fire on the starboard side. The starboard wing dropped and it went into the sea from 200 feet.

I was flying through the barrage from the Fleet when I saw five aircraft diving from approximately 3,000 feet. I climbed to 2,000 feet and did a beam attack ending upon the quarter

117

at 50 yards. I saw the pilot's cockpit shatter and the angle of dive changed from 65° to 85° and go straight into the sea. I followed him down but could not continue firing as I had no ammunition left. When the aircraft hit the sea I saw the air gunner begin to climb out. It was later confirmed that the pilot was badly injured but the air gunner was OK.

In any case the damage to the carrier had come too late to help the Axis cause. Thanks to the protection afforded by the Fleet Air Arm fighters, the most determined of attacks had been able to sink only one of the precious merchantmen. The value of that protection would only be emphasized by the events of that night and the next day when it was no longer available. The subsequent fate of the convoy makes sad reading as the enemy rained blow after blow upon it, the vital, vulnerable tanker receiving particular attention.

But the 'good start' proved just good enough. On the evening of 13 August three freighters arrived at Malta. A fourth which had been damaged and had proceeded independently joined them next day. And early on the 15th it seemed that the entire population of Malta was there to roar a welcome as the unconquerable *Ohio*, totally disabled, desperately low in the water, but with her essential cargo intact, was towed into Grand Harbour. Her master Captain Mason was awarded the George Cross. The island which he and his ship had done so much to save had won the same recognition four months earlier.

If the Sea Hurricanes had done nothing else they would still have justified their existence, but almost exactly a month later they would again play a decisive part in defending another important convoy route. In July 1942 Convoy PQ 17, making for Russia, had been ordered to scatter in the belief that it was threatened by a German surface force, and twenty-three freighters, a tanker and a rescue ship had then been massacred by air attacks or U-boats. The next Russian convoy, PQ 18, was planned for September – it was essential that most of the forty merchant vessels that it contained should get through.

The task of ensuring this was entrusted to Rear Admiral Robert Burnett who commanded the cruiser *Scylla*, eighteen destroyers and the escort carrier *Avenger* on which were eighteen Sea Hurricanes of 802 and 883 Squadrons. His enemies gave the task of preventing it to both U-boats and aircraft. The former would sink three freighters at the heavy cost of three of their own number, but the principal effort would be made by the ninety-two torpedo-planes and 133 long-range bombers available to the Luftwaffe.

There were three major air attacks on PQ 18 and they might have been orchestrated to show the value of fighter protection. The first took place on 13 September. The Sea Hurricanes drove away a small group of Junkers Ju 88s but while they were so engaged a perfectly timed assault by over forty torpedo-bombers, which was thus opposed only by AA fire, sank no less than eight merchantmen, an ammunition ship disintegrating in a horrific detonation.

Happily the two big attacks on the 14th had different results. The *Avenger* would not be distracted a second time, and perhaps the enemy realized this, since their initial raid was directed against the little carrier. As Admiral Burnett would later record:

> It was a fine sight to see *Avenger* peeling off Hurricanes whilst streaking across the front of the convoy from starboard to port . . . and then being chased by torpedo-bombers as she steamed down on the opposite course to the convoy.

No hits were scored in this attack but the Luftwaffe quickly mounted another one, again aimed mainly at *Avenger*, though in the convoy another ammunition ship simply vanished in a vast column of fire and smoke. The attackers were met by every anti-aircraft gun that could be brought to bear, and also by the Sea Hurricanes which followed their targets right through the full fury of the barrage. Three of them were in fact shot down by this, but thankfully all the airmen were picked up safely. Admiral Burnett continues:

> I shall never forget the reckless gallantry of the naval pilots in their determination to get in among the enemy despite the solid mass of our defensive fire.

119

During the course of their raids on PQ 18, the Germans, by their own admission, lost over forty warplanes destroyed or damaged beyond repair. A large majority of these fell to AA fire but *Avenger*'s Sea Hurricanes shot down three Heinkel He 111s and two Junkers Ju 88s for certain. They also damaged at least seventeen other aircraft. How many of these failed to return to base, or were written off on arrival, or, unable to manoeuvre properly, became easy victims for the ships' gunners, will never be known; it matters little in any case for the interceptors' main value lay not in downing individual aeroplanes but in breaking up enemy formations. It was the guns and the fighters in combination which gained the victory on 14 September.

It was a substantial victory too. No later Arctic convoy would face anything like the same weight of air attack; indeed shortly thereafter the Germans would transfer the bulk of their torpedo-bombers to the Mediterranean. Even in the case of PQ 18 the losses incurred so discouraged the Luftwaffe that 15 September saw only small sporadic raids by high-level bombers which caused no damage. On the afternoon of the 16th most of the escorts, including *Avenger*, left to guard a returning QP convoy, but even with the carrier gone the Luftwaffe managed to sink only one more ship. Twenty-seven reached Russia, carrying, as the enemy openly acknowledged, sufficient tanks, vehicles, aircraft and other war materials 'to equip a whole new army for the front'.

One other reason for PQ 18's comparative immunity after *Avenger*'s departure was that it was still protected by a Sea Hurricane – a Sea Hurricane IA to be precise. It can be argued that such aircraft were not really Sea Hurricanes at all since they could not land on carriers but they did take off from ships at sea, and considering that their duties were the most remarkable that even Hurricane pilots were ever called on to perform, they provide a fitting conclusion to the Sea Hurricane story.

The Mark IA – also known as the 'Catafighter' or the 'Hurricat' for reasons which will soon become apparent – was originally designed to deal with the menace of the Focke-Wulf Fw 200C Condor. This was a huge four-engined bomber with a vast range which could strike at convoys in the Atlantic far beyond the reach of shore-based fighters. It could also track convoys for hours,

120

sending a constant stream of information to the U-boat 'wolf-packs', while circling out of range of AA guns; indeed there is an amusing, if improbable story of a convoy commodore signalling a request to the Focke-Wulf to fly the other way round as he was getting giddy watching it.

In the absence of aircraft-carriers, it was felt that the only way of dealing with this problem was to adapt merchantmen so that in addition to their normal cargo they could carry a 70-foot long steel ramp. On this a converted Hurricane I would be mounted and from this it would be catapulted by means of thirteen rocket motors which produced a speed of 75 mph at the moment the Hurricane became airborne. Even an aircraft as robust as the Hurricane had to be modified for this purpose, the fuselage for instance being strengthened, while among other alterations was a heavily-padded head-rest against which the pilot could lean in order to absorb the shock of launching. Unfortunately the modifications did reduce the speed of the Hurricats to only about 245 mph at 3,000 feet, which was only 10 mph more than the top speed of a Condor.

In all, thirty-five vessels were so converted. They were known as CAM-ships, the initials standing for Catapult Aircraft Merchantman. To fly the Hurricane, the RAF asked for volunteers, which is not surprising for it is difficult to imagine the cool nerve required to be a Hurricat pilot. In addition to the risk of their ship being sunk under them, as several were, there were the dangers involved in any air combat and they would rarely have the fuel required to enable them to reach land. Consequently they would have either to bale out into the icy waters of the North Atlantic, or later the Arctic, where they risked freezing to death in short order, or to 'ditch', whereupon the Hurricane's large radiator would often drag it under in a matter of seconds. Nonetheless there proved no shortage of intrepid characters willing to face these obvious hazards, whether out of a wish for excitement, a desire for change, or perhaps a feeling that the task was of such importance as to justify the risks.

Nor did the Royal Navy show a fraction less commitment than the Royal Air Force. It provided almost all the CAM-ships with Fighter Direction Officers who guided the airmen to their targets, and their radar operators. In addition it arranged the conversion of a handful of auxiliary vessels, known as Fighter Catapult Ships, for 'catafighting' work. These flew the white ensign and were manned by naval personnel; the aircraft were flown by Fleet Air Arm pilots from 804 Squadron who, amazingly, were not volunteers but simply detailed for these dangerous duties on normal appointments. In practice, however, only one of the FC-ships carried Hurricanes, the others being given Fulmars, which proved quite unsuited for the purpose. The exception was HMS *Maplin*, a converted, fast banana boat, from which the very first operational Hurricat launching was soon to take place.

This occurred on 18 July 1941, but before the Sea Hurricane's pilot, Lieutenant Robert Everett, could engage a Condor attacking a convoy, the enemy warplane was shot down by anti-aircraft fire, greatly to the delight of the merchantmen but somewhat to the disappointment of Everett. At least the lack of combat meant that he had enough fuel to fly to the British Isles, which he duly reached after being airborne for just under two hours.

'Bob' Everett was one of the most interesting of all the men who flew Hurricanes. Forty years old, he had been born in Australia, had farmed in South Africa, and had then moved to Britain, where he learned to fly, spending his summers as a charter pilot and his winters as a professional National Hunt jockey. Considered both brave and reliable, he partnered a big ungainly chestnut named Gregalach – of whom exactly the same could have been said; they made a worthy pair – to win the 1929 Grand National out of a record field of sixty-six. He stated without hesitation though that nothing could match the excitements of 'catafighting' and in this role his finest moment lay just ahead on 3 August, when he again flew off *Maplin* to attack a Condor:

I got within one and a half miles of the Focke-Wulf before it seemed to notice my presence. I intercepted it after nine minutes flying and ranged up alongside at 600 yards and slightly above it. When my machine was slightly ahead of its starboard quarter the stern cannon opened fire. These rounds passed underneath or fell short of the Hurricane. It took quite

122

an appreciable time to get abeam and the for'ard cannon was also firing – again the rounds passed underneath or short. The Focke-Wulf then turned sharply to port, but seemed to change its mind and turned back on its original course. By this time I had reached its starboard bow and three machine-guns opened up, as well as the for'ard cannon. I did a quick turn to port and opened fire just abaft the beam. I fired five-second bursts all the way until I was 40 yards astern of the enemy. Another short burst at this range and my guns were empty. I noticed pieces flying off the starboard side of the Focke-Wulf and it appeared to be alight inside the fuselage. (Everett's Combat Report)

The Condor in fact was fatally hit. Dropping a wing, it plunged into the sea. Everett returned in triumph to the convoy where he 'ditched'. The Hurricane turned over but Everett struggled free and was picked up unhurt to receive a well-earned DSO. He was lost almost six months later when engine failure on a routine flight brought his machine down near the Isle of Anglesey. His body was washed ashore later.

There would be nine further Hurricat launchings, one more from *Maplin*, the rest from the CAM-ships. The pilots would engage not only Condors but also Heinkel He 111s and Junkers Ju 88s attacking the Arctic convoys. To give an example, Convoy PQ 18 had a Sea Hurricane guard even after the *Avenger* had turned back. On 18 September 1942, a Hurricat piloted by Flying Officer 'Jack' Burr was flown off *Empire Morn* to oppose a formation of fifteen Heinkel He 111s carrying torpedoes:

I dived on them and carried out a head-on and port beam attack on a He 111 opening fire at 300 yards and closing to 150 yards. I noticed my shots striking the engine and nose of the Heinkel and as I turned above and behind to the left I noticed white smoke coming from his starboard engine. I closed again to 250 yards and gave him the rest of my ammunition in a beam attack carried out from his starboard side. I then noticed that white smoke was coming from both his engines. (Burr's Combat Report)

Intelligence assessments later credited Burr with a confirmed 'kill', and he remained over the convoy so that he could make mock attacks on any other enemy formation that showed up. When none did, he decided to fly to the aerodrome at Keg Ostrov near Archangel, finally landing there after a flight of almost 240 miles, with five gallons of petrol left in his reserve tank.

Altogether the pilots of the Sea Hurricane IAs destroyed seven enemy aircraft (including Everett's and Burr's victims) and damaged at least three more, losing only one of their own number and that not through any fault in man or machine but because a parachute did not open sufficiently. Even more important than this high strike rate was the Hurricanes' value as a deterrent, particularly against the once-feared Condors. These all but abandoned their bombing raids and greatly reduced their reconnaissance activities. There was no longer any question of their following a convoy; on the contrary the mere sight of a CAM-ship would result in their abrupt departure, depriving the U-boats of any detailed information and thus saving countless lives.

Not that this gained the Condors any immunity. On 1 November 1942, for instance, Flying Officer Norman Taylor from the *Empire Heath* shot down a Condor despite having his Hurricane's port wing riddled with bullets. On his return to the convoy, where he was greeted by the sirens of every single ship, Taylor baled out safely – only to find that his dinghy would not inflate. Happily his life-jacket kept him afloat until he could be rescued. He was awarded a DFC, which seems especially well deserved considering he was a non-swimmer – a fact he had carefully omitted to mention when volunteering as a Hurricat pilot.

On 15 July 1943 the Merchant Ship Fighter Unit, to give the Hurricats their formal title, was officially disbanded, to the accompaniment of a generous signal from the Admiralty expressing 'great appreciation' of its services. Yet, oddly enough, this did not mark the end of the Sea Hurricane IA's achievements. Two CAM-ships, *Empire Darwin* and *Empire Tide*, were still at sea, escorting a convoy from Gibraltar. On 28 July this was attacked by Condors and both vessels launched their Hurricats.

First aloft was Pilot Officer Stewart from *Empire Darwin*, whose sortie was witnessed by, among others, Second Officer

Francis of the freighter *City of Exeter*. In Ralph Barker's book *The Hurricats* – which of course deals in detail with this particular aspect of the Hurricane's war – Francis relates how:

> This aircraft [Stewart's] flew off from the convoy then passed ahead of it, chasing a Focke-Wulf to the port quarter in an anti-clockwise direction. The Hurricane dived on the Fw 200 which dropped sharply, rose again for a moment, and crashed into the sea.

Stewart next drove away a second Condor which dropped its bombs at random before departing in haste. Then Pilot Officer Flynn from *Empire Tide* joined the fight and although his Hurricane was badly damaged by return fire, he left a third Condor losing height, with smoke pouring from one engine. Intelligence reports indicate that it failed to return to base. Both Hurricat pilots baled out and survived their ordeals.

For ordeals they were, and if it is thought that the pilots of the Sea Hurricane IAs have received disproportionate notice, the reason is that their exploits epitomize those of the Hurricane pilots in general. They were called on to carry out unusual, difficult, dangerous, important tasks, but thanks to their own skill and courage, and the versatility and reliability of their Hurricanes, they did carry them out – with the maximum of success and the minimum loss of life.

NOTES
1 All *Eagle*'s Sea Hurricanes went down with her apart from the four aloft at the time, and of these all except Hutton's were lost in the later stages of the operation.
2 In fact, Popham had landed on *Victorious*, not his own *Indomitable*.

Chapter 10

The Onslaught of Japan

Far greater loss of life would be suffered and perhaps greater ordeals would be endured by those Hurricane pilots who were hastily sent to the Far East when, on 7 December 1941, a new enemy – brave, capable, resolute, ruthless and all the more dangerous for being badly underrated – exploded into the conflict. That the Japanese onslaught also added the United States to the list of combatants would ultimately ensure the Allies' triumph, but for the next five months Britain and the United States were able to do little more than console each other for their mutual misfortunes.

One reason for the Allies' lack of respect for their latest foe was that they knew very little about the Japanese. Their information with regard to Japan's warplanes was particularly vague, being made worse by that country's complicated system of aircraft classification. To solve this problem, it was decided to give each type an arbitrary code name, the bombers having ladies' names, the fighters men's names. Even that was disregarded in one important instance, for in spite of an official code name of 'Zeke', the Japanese Navy's finest fighter was almost always known as the Mitsubishi Zero or, to RAF pilots, as the Navy Nought.

This latter name serves as a reminder that the aircraft was a naval one. In consequence, though accounts at the time and for many years afterwards, constantly referred to every Japanese fighter as a Zero – perhaps in unconscious tribute to its excellence – the Hurricane pilots in the Far East were normally faced by

Japanese Army Air Force fighters, the Nakajima Ki 27 'Nate' or Ki 43 'Oscar'. These, like the Zero, were small, agile machines but they were slower and, lacking the Zero's cannons, did not have the same firepower. Nonetheless they proved worthy opponents, particularly when flown by airmen with long experience of Japan's war with China. To the RAF pilots who had been assured that Japanese aeroplanes were mere imitations of Western ones, but some five years out of date, their effectiveness came as a horrible surprise.

So much was this the case that it brought about an equally false reaction which declared that Hurricanes were considerably inferior to their opponents. Terence Kelly, who as a young sergeant pilot was a member of 258 Squadron, the second Hurricane unit to reach the Far East, was not one who held this opinion. In his *Hurricane and Spitfire Pilots at War* he declares bluntly:

I have read book after book in which this nonsense about the superiority of the Japanese fighters is written. It simply was not so. The Hurricane was not outclassed by the Zero, or as we knew it the Navy O or Navy Nought, nor by the Hayabusa [the 'Oscar']. The Hurricane was at least the match of either machine and had the battles between them been fought on equal terms would have coped quite comfortably. Such was my opinion at the time and so it remains to the present day . . .

As to the qualities of the two aircraft, the Zero certainly had advantages. It was more manoeuvrable, it was marginally faster up to heights of about fifteen thousand feet and it had a far longer range . . . The Hurricane for its part had several very distinct advantages. It had a better ceiling, the aircraft could take punishment which would have made the lightly built Zero disintegrate, it was faster at high altitudes and the pilot had the protection of resealing petrol tanks and an armour plate shield behind his back . . .

. . . The Japanese pilots [were also unable] . . . to follow the Hurricanes down [in a dive] because beyond a certain speed (which . . . the Hurricanes could accept with ease) the Zeros' wings would simply have folded up.

These comments were even more appropriate with regard to the Japanese Army fighters which, as mentioned earlier, were less dangerous than the Zero. Unfortunately no such information was available for the benefit of 232 Squadron which reached Singapore on 13 January 1942. Its aircraft were Hurricane Mark Is or early IIAs which, having originally been destined for the Middle East, were handicapped by desert air filters. Its real handicap, however, was its pilots' ignorance of both the virtues and the defects of Japanese warplanes. Being used to the Hurricane's ability to outmanoeuvre any other monoplane fighter in Europe, they tried to dog-fight with their nimble foes, whereas their best tactics would have been to attack these from above, then dive away out of trouble. Many fine men lost their lives needlessly while these lessons were being learned.

Nonetheless 232 Squadron still proved able to inflict considerable casualties on the Japanese bombers – if seldom so spectacularly as is revealed in this Combat Report for 21 January by Flight Lieutenant Farthing, which is recorded in *Bloody Shambles* by Christopher Shores and Brian Cull with Yasuho Izawa:[1]

There were about 30 of them [Mitsubishi 'Nell' bombers] flying a few feet above us, and another lot higher still. We went in against the first batch on a beam attack, selecting a formation of three. I picked one and gave him a fairly long burst, and travelled ahead of him a few hundred yards. There was a terrific explosion behind me, and as I turned back I saw there was a big gap in the enemy formation.[2] I actually flew through a wall of smoke and burning machine debris.

I turned on to another of the enemy and gave him a squirt of fire. He went down in a dive after a piece of the tailplane had broken away, followed by bits and pieces of engine. By then my machine was giving trouble and I had to land. When I landed it was found that the engine intake was full of bits and pieces of Japanese aircraft, presumably from the first victim which blew up in the air.

Sadly such successes could scarcely challenge the Japanese command of the air which was based on overwhelming numbers.

And in any case by the time 232 Squadron arrived it was already too late to check the irresistible advance of the Japanese Army – though the Hurricane pilots did do their best to hamper the enemy on the ground as well. Their efforts were generously acknowledged by Colonel Masanobu Tsuji, the enemy's Director of Military Operations, who in *Singapore: The Japanese Version* relates that:

> The Hurricanes flying low over the rubber forest were a serious challenge. Their intrepid pilots continually machine-gunned our roads, shooting up our motor transport and blocking traffic . . . Until then our mobile corps had been advancing on the paved roads in broad daylight taking no precautions against enemy air raids. While the Hurricanes were flying even single cars moved off the road into the cover of the jungle, and all convoys had to move off the road and get out of sight at the first alarm.

Colonel Tsuji was right to use the word 'intrepid' for the Japanese troops were well protected by plentiful AA batteries. On 9 February for instance, the American Flying Officer Arthur Donahue and the New Zealander Sergeant 'Bill' Moodie of 258 Squadron – which had reached Singapore on 31 January, having flown off the deck of the carrier *Indomitable* – encountered heavy flak while in low-level pursuit of an enemy aircraft. At almost the same time Donahue sighted an Oscar which he attacked, apparently without effect, before pulling up sharply, just missing the treetops. In his book *Last Flight from Singapore*,[3] he describes what happened next:

> I turned left to get around at any new enemies that might be behind. And there, amid the confusion of anti-aircraft fire bursting all around, I saw Sergeant M—'s [Moodie's] Hurricane diving steeply, obviously hit! I was right over him as he struck, in the corner of a little field, at close to three hundred miles an hour, in a terrible ghastly eruption of splintered wings and flying pieces and then steam and dust and smoke that swirled out to obscure the awful sight . . .
> . . . [Returning to base] I had to give them the news of

Sergeant M—'s [Moodie's] death. I hadn't known him well, but the mute faces and glistening eyes of some of the boys told me how much they thought of him. I wondered if any of them felt it was my fault.

Less than a week later, on 15 February, Singapore surrendered together with 70,000 troops – but not the remaining pilots of 232 and 258 Squadrons who had already retired to Sumatra. Here they were joined by reinforcements which, like 258 Squadron earlier, had flown off HMS *Indomitable*. And here, operating from two airfields – P1 just north of the capital Palembang and P2, a secret base in the jungle some 20 miles to the south – they resumed their hopeless struggle.

'Hopeless' because not only were the Hurricanes heavily outnumbered, but they were flying from inadequate landing surfaces, there was no radar system, the Observer Corps posts were much too widely scattered and in the absence of Very High Frequency (VHF) radio sets there was practically no ground-to-air communication, and very little between individual aircraft. The inevitable result was that the Hurricanes never received adequate warning of enemy raids and at P1 at least were constantly being engaged when either taking off or landing. Terence Kelly describes one of these raids on 13 February in his account of his own experiences, *Hurricane Over the Jungle*:

The only one they caught was Sergeant Scott. He was well into his final approach, at perhaps two hundred feet, in fact about level with me still in my aircraft taxying in. I saw with horror a Navy Nought[4] on his tail . . . I saw smoke begin to pour from Scotty's engine and I could even see his head as he hauled back on his stick to give himself height to bale out – and in fact he did succeed and jumping from the aircraft at eight or nine hundred feet landed by parachute safely near the airfield.

What was more remarkable was what happened to the Navy O. Its speed in the attack could not have been very great, three or four hundred miles an hour perhaps, and even the recovery from the dive with more than a hundred and fifty feet of airspace in hand not remarkably severe; yet it was more than the airframe could stand. Both wings simply folded upwards like the wings of carrier-borne aircraft which fold for stacking purposes and the Navy Nought crashed beside us in the jungle.

Nor were these raids the only danger from the air. On 14 February the Japanese sprang a complete surprise in the form of parachute landings, one of which was dangerously close to P1, necessitating the abandonment of the base and the destruction of a number of Hurricanes rendered unserviceable by the poor conditions. Next day Japanese soldiers, packed together in large barges, moved up the Musi River towards Palembang. Unaware of the existence of P2, and confident that they would be exempt from interference from the air, they would be grimly disillusioned. The few remaining Hurricanes savaged them without mercy. One sortie was made by 258 Squadron's two authors, Flying Officer Donahue and Sergeant Kelly, and the latter confirms that:

It was carnage . . .

I probably saw the effect of Donahue's attack much better than any of my own because I had fallen astern behind him waiting my turn and with nothing to do and not much to think about but watch.

The flicker of the defending gunners was like torches switched on and off but no more than that. We had orbited to get straight in line and dived from perhaps a thousand feet. I really don't believe Donahue missed a barge, his guns raking the convoy from head to stern. The bullets made an unforgettable pattern. There was a pincushion of water ahead of the nearest barge which moved along so that as the bullets raked through a barge what one saw was the pinpoints of light in the barge itself which would have been the tracers striking and the pincushioning carrying along both sides of the barges and then reappearing in between each barge. And so on along the line.

It is impossible to conceive the horror and the slaughter wrought.

But there were not nearly enough Hurricanes on hand to halt the Japanese completely. Palembang fell next day and although P2 had still not been located by the enemy, it was felt that its position was now too precarious. The survivors of 232 and 258 Squadrons retreated once more, this time to Java, where they changed their identities, to the confusion of later reports.

What happened was that the ground crews from 242 and 605 Squadrons had now reached Java – though not their pilots who had gone to help defend Malta. It was decided to evacuate the exhausted ground crews from 232 and 258 Squadrons and allocate the flying personnel to these new squadrons. Most of 258 Squadron's pilots left as well but a few joined 605 Squadron together with some from 488 Squadron, a New Zealand unit that had previously flown obsolete Brewster Buffalo fighters in Malaya. The pilots of 232 Squadron transferred their allegiance en masse to 242 Squadron.

There was also a third Hurricane unit in Java. Twenty-four Mark Is had earlier arrived on the island in crates and these were handed over to pilots of the Dutch Java Air Force. They also received the services of some RAF ground crews and an Engineer Officer. In Robert Jackson's *Hawker Hurricane*, Squadron Leader John David describes how:

> The Hurricane was an eye-opener for them and they revelled in its speed (!),[5] rate of climb and, above all, its armament and toughness . . .
>
> The Hurricanes' first operation was a total success, because eight of them – all we could get into the air – caught a formation of Japanese Navy single-engined carrier aircraft (probably 'Kates') returning unescorted after a maximum-range trip and shot the lot down. That was their only easy one; after that it was nearly always fighter to fighter. We were lucky to get five minutes warning of a raid coming in, and we were usually at a disadvantage.
>
> The Dutch were, however, brilliant pilots, . . . and the strength of the Hurricane allowed them to take ridiculous liberties with it. Some of our repairs were ridiculous too, including using the village bicycle repairer (Chinese) to braize

damage to the fuselage trusses and the ladies (Javanese) to provide patches for fabric repair.

Inevitably, we irritated the Japanese too much and they located our airfield, which was cutting up badly, and mounted a major low-level bombing and strafing attack just after our morning patrol had come in. Six aircraft were re-fuelling and all were destroyed when the petrol bowsers brewed up.

Other raids quickly followed and the remaining Dutch Hurricanes were eliminated; the RAF Hurricanes lasted only a little longer. By 7 March just two were left and these were destroyed on the ground next day. Prior to this, however, Terence Kelly had had a remarkable experience which he shares with us in *Hurricane Over the Jungle*. By now the pilots were aware that their best course when opposed by enemy fighters was to engage them from above, then dive away as steeply as possible. Unfortunately Kelly took the tactic rather too far:

I must have dived vertically at full throttle for seven or eight thousand feet and when I tried to start easing out, I found there was nothing I could do. The controls were frozen solid . . .

It was obvious that baling out wasn't any good – at the sort of speed I'd by now reached, probably terminal velocity, if I'd even managed to get my head out of the cockpit it would have been torn off and even if it wasn't the tail fin would probably just about slice me in two. So that wasn't on. And if I couldn't do anything with the stick there was only one thing left – the tail trim.

In a Hurricane there were minute strips of metal like tiny elevators on the trailing edges of the elevators themselves which were adjustable by turning a relatively large wheel inside the cockpit. Like the smallest weights on a balance, these strips could be moved fractionally to give perfect fore and aft balance so that in normal flight the stick is absolutely neutral – indeed that is their purpose. One was always instructed to treat tail trim with great respect and it was often

133

said that misuse at high speeds could tear off the tailplane. Now it was Hobson's choice.

I took one hand off the stick and wound the trim wheel the merest fraction towards myself and at once grabbing at the stick again hauled on it with all my strength. And I was rewarded by the faintest softness, the slightest yielding . . . [Repeating the action] I knew I was going to be all right – that I had left the vertical . . . I began to see the red and green world below which had been fixed begin to slide away behind me as the nose came up, all the time accelerating until at length there was the horizon and I was flying straight and level.

I reversed the trim, busy talking to myself as I found I always did under these kind of circumstances. I looked at the altimeter – fifteen thousand feet. Quite a long dive. I looked at the airspeed indicator and couldn't believe my eyes . . . How could I be doing only three hundred odd miles an hour after what must have been a dive of terminal velocity . . . The speed was dropping fast – as it should, I told myself aloud, throttled right back as I was. And it was then, of course, that the penny dropped. I'd gone right round the clock not once, but twice! I watched it absolutely fascinated, seeing it complete a counter revolution, pass through the four hundred miles an hour at one o'clock on the inner scale and then through two hundred and forty miles an hour at five o'clock on the outer one. It should, I thought, be all right now. I pushed the throttle open experimentally and after a moment or two the airspeed began to pick up again.

There is a rule of thumb for converting true flying speed from the speed indicated by the instruments which, working on air pressure, underwrite your speed the higher you climb. You add for every thousand feet of height one and three quarter per cent to the indicated speed. Even by the time I was flying straight and level I had been flying at more than five hundred and ninety miles an hour. The vertical speed must have been knocking the speed of sound.

It is a remarkable achievement for the designer of an aircraft with a top straight and level speed of about three hundred and thirty miles an hour that it could be put to such a test and emerge triumphant; it seemed that much more remarkable when compared with the disintegration of its rival at Palembang.

There was no doubt about it, I thought, as I flew along, looking affectionately at the sturdy wings with their rows of rivets – as [Sergeant] Arthur Sheerin had once said to me, 'She's a sweet, bloody marvellous, wonderful kite.'

Those pilots who flew Hurricanes in Burma must have held similar views. There too they were faced with heavy adverse odds, operated from unsuitable airfields and were backed by an inadequate warning system – yet their aircrafts' virtues enabled them to take a heavy toll of their foes and have a fair chance of surviving the inevitable repercussions. A good example of the Hurricane's value in both these aspects of air combat is given by Messrs Shores and Cull in *Bloody Shambles*,[6] quoting the experience of Pilot Officer Guy Underwood of 135 Squadron on 6 February 1942:

I hit one Japanese aircraft[7] as he was climbing up – a quarter frontal attack – his aircraft bursting into flames (this was later confirmed by one of our pilots); a second dive gave me another chance and I saw bullets from my aircraft strike another fighter in a quarter attack from astern but in this case the pilot was either killed or took very rapid evasive action (this was claimed as a probable).

On a further dive, however, I saw a Japanese aircraft almost head on and as I passed him in the opposite direction I could see his aircraft pulling round in a hard turn and very close to me. Almost immediately afterwards bullets hit the rear of my aircraft – presumably from that particular aircraft – and my cockpit canopy disappeared (presumably shot off) and I received what seemed to be a kick in the back of my left leg . . .

On landing, an examination of the aircraft showed that besides the lost canopy, bullet holes were present in the rear fuselage and the top of the rudder had been shot off. My leg wound turned out to be the apparent result of an explosive bullet hitting something in the aircraft and then dispersing its bits rather like buckshot in the back of the leg.

The most successful Hurricane pilot at this time was 135 Squadron's CO, Squadron Leader Frank Carey. He had already gained distinction flying with another famous Hurricane squadron, No. 43, in the Battle of Britain, and he now added to this by being credited with the destruction of at least ten Japanese aircraft during this period, including three in one day on 26 February.

Yet as in Malaya and the East Indies, so it was in Burma. Whatever the successes in the air, nothing could stop the Japanese soldiers on the ground. As they closed in on Rangoon – which had to be abandoned on 7 March – the Hurricanes were forced out of their nearby base at Mingaladon. 135 Squadron went to Akyab Island off the north-west coast of Burma, but another Hurricane squadron, No. 17, moved to Magwe in central Burma. Here it was joined by nine Blenheims and from here on 21 March both bombers and fighters delivered a spectacular raid on Mingaladon, now occupied by Japanese warplanes. One member of 17 Squadron who took part was the Canadian Pilot Officer Hedley Everard; his account also appears in *Bloody Shambles*:

The sun's first rays were almost parallel to the airfield runway as we made our first strafing attack. My task was to silence an ack-ack position on the northern approach. As I closed the range to 600 yards, I was able to see the half dozen members of the gun crew sitting on a low wall of sandbags. They were knocked over by my initial burst.

I performed a climbing-diving turn towards a line of fighters parked wing-tip to wing-tip along the runway, some of which were already smoking from the initial surprise attack by my fellow flyers. I carefully sighted my burst at the first machine in the line, but had obviously fired out of range since the bullets clammed short of the target.

As I flashed overhead, I looked down into the cockpit and caught the bland curious stare of the Japanese pilot who was being helped to strap in by his crewman. It was incredible. They had ignored my murderous attack.

I swung around for a second pass. By now the pilot had started his engine and was just beginning to move towards the runway. With deadly purpose now, my bullets riddled the engine and cockpit. The aircraft slewed up on its nose as I passed overhead. I glimpsed the pilot slumped in his seat.

I glanced at the runway and saw my buddies picking off the fighters as they vainly attempted to take off. [Then] the Squadron Leader [Squadron Leader Stone] spotted some Japanese fighters rising from other satellite airfields nearby and gave the order to return to base.

In one sense, however, the attack had been too successful. Stung into violent action, the Japanese on that same afternoon sent wave after wave of aircraft against Magwe which they reduced to a blazing ruin. The few Hurricanes that survived struggled off to join their fellows at Akyab, but that base also was now subjected to a whole sequence of raids. The remnants of the Hurricane units left for India, and the Japanese, now with total command of the air, proceeded with their relentless occupation of the whole of Burma.

To protect the flank of their advancing armies, the Japanese Navy struck into the Bay of Bengal. Five aircraft-carriers, all of which had taken part in the Pearl Harbour mission, were directed against Ceylon, where they were to attack the great port of Colombo, the Royal Navy base at Trincomalee, and any units of the British Fleet that they might encounter. At the time the enemy had no intention of following up with a landing on Ceylon, although this could have brought rich strategic gains in the possible severance of vital Allied supply routes: those to Allied forces on the Burma frontier through the Bay of Bengal; those to Allied forces in North Africa through the Indian Ocean; and those carrying oil to India from the Middle East through the Arabian Sea. Accordingly a strong school of thought at Japan's Naval General Staff did favour mounting an invasion, particularly if their carriers met no real resistance.

It was fortunate, therefore, that resistance was encountered. The Royal Navy, which was considerably weaker than the enemy strike force, had retired to Addu Atoll, a secret base in the Maldive Islands 600 miles to the south-west, and the Japanese sank a number of vessels detached from the main body, including the little carrier *Hermes* and cruisers *Dorsetshire* and *Cornwall*. The assaults on Colombo and Trincomalee, by contrast, did meet determined opposition. The latter was guarded by the Hurricanes of 261 Squadron, under the South African Squadron Leader Lewis, which had flown off HMS *Indomitable*; the former by the Hurricanes of Squadron Leader Chater's 30 Squadron from *Indomitable* and of a revived 258 Squadron, led by the Rhodesian Squadron Leader Fletcher, which had been transferred from India.

Colombo was the first to be attacked on 5 April. No adequate warning was given by radar and the pilots of 30 Squadron took off amid bursting bombs, only to be attacked by genuine Zeros before they could gain height. Eight aircraft and five airmen were lost. 258 Squadron was more fortunate, as it was stationed at a landing ground that had been constructed on a racecourse, the existence of which the Japanese were unaware. Unfortunately the Hurricanes made the common mistake of trying to dog-fight with the Zeros. In *The Most Dangerous Moment*,[8] Michael Tomlinson includes this description by Flight Lieutenant 'Teddy' Peacock-Edwards, who like his CO was a Rhodesian, of the action which earned him a DFC:

> I managed to shoot down one Navy 99 [a 'Val' dive-bomber] into the sea . . . but by this time it was every man for himself and the escorting fighters had come down . . . I was set upon by enemy fighters which I managed to shake off by climbing, but I was followed by two of these and when I found myself in a superior position proceeded to attack the one I con- sidered to be in the most vulnerable position. I followed him down but did not finally observe the results of my attack as I was again set upon by half a dozen fighters.
>
> This time the position was such that my tactics developed into a game of hide and seek in and around the palm trees. At this altitude the Hurricane was at a distinct disadvantage as opposed to the Navy O. And while four of them held off at a safe height, two continued to carry out head-on and stern

attacks on me. I managed to get in some good bursts on the aircraft doing the head-on attacks but the battle was drawing to a close and I observed no definite results. The aircraft was damaged and it is quite possible that it never regained its carrier base.

The end finally came when I was forced to crash-land in a paddy field. During the impact I must have been dazed because I woke up sitting in a pile of wreckage.

Dazed or not, Peacock-Edwards was one more pilot who owed his life to the strength of his Hurricane, but 258 Squadron lost a total of nine aircraft and five pilots. The two Hurricane squadrons between them had downed five Vals and one Zero. Nine other Japanese aircraft had been damaged.

It was a similar story when the enemy attacked Trincomalee on 9 April. Hopelessly outnumbered, ten of 261 Squadron's Hurricanes were shot down or crash-landed, though only two of their pilots were killed. They destroyed two Kate high-level bombers and one Zero, and damaged ten more bombers; two further Zeros fell to AA fire. At both Colombo and Trincomalee, however, comparatively little damage was done to port facilities or shipping and, best of all, the Japanese did not feel justified in changing their plans so as to include a landing in Ceylon. Their carriers had thus gained no strategic benefit; instead they had wasted several weeks when they could have been countering the American build-up in the Pacific – to which ocean they now belatedly returned.

The threat to Ceylon was never renewed, and although sporadic air raids kept the RAF on the defensive in India for a while, the 'most dangerous moment' had passed. Soon it would be the Hurricane pilots who would go onto the offensive. As they would do in North Africa. And as they had long been accustomed to do across the English Channel.

NOTES
1 The full title is *Bloody Shambles: The First Comprehensive Account of Air Operations Over South-East Asia December 1941–April 1942. Volume One: The Drift to War to the Fall of Singapore.*

2 It was confirmed by other pilots that the exploding bomber had brought down two more which had been flying close behind it; they crashed in flames.

3 This was published posthumously after Donahue, by then a squadron leader, had died in action over the English Channel on 11 September 1942.

4 Japanese accounts confirm that the fighter in question was in fact not a Navy Nought but an Army Oscar.

5 The criticism implied by the exclamation mark was not entirely justified. A Hurricane I, even when handicapped by a desert filter, could match the speed of the Japanese Army's Nates and Oscars. Unfortunately the Dutchmen's opponents on most occasions were Zeros which, as we have seen, were faster than any Hurricane, at least at low altitudes.

6 Volume Two: *The Defence of Sumatra to the Fall of Burma.*

7 Underwood's opponents were Army Nate fighters.

8 This title derives from a comment made by Churchill during a visit to Washington in March 1946. He told Mr Lester Pearson, later Prime Minister of Canada but then Canadian Ambassador to the United States, that 'the most dangerous moment of the war' and the one which caused him 'the greatest alarm' was when the Japanese threatened Ceylon. Had the Japanese followed their sortie with a landing, his alarm would probably have been justified.

Chapter 11

Conflict across the Channel

On New Year's Day 1941, three Hurricanes from 1 Squadron crossed the French coast. They were led by Flight Lieutenant Clowes who was mentioned earlier as a sergeant pilot in 1939 but had earned rapid promotion since – he would command his own Hurricane squadron, No. 79, by the end of the year, and would finish the war as a wing commander. His section spent twenty minutes strafing enemy positions between Calais and Boulogne, unhindered by hostile fighters.

Such operations by just a few Hurricanes at a time were mysteriously known as 'Rhubarbs' and would continue throughout 1941 into 1942. They suffered a number of casualties which were the more serious because even if a pilot baled out, he would still be lost to the RAF as a prisoner of war. Nonetheless they gained some intangible but important benefits. They forced the Luftwaffe to adopt an increasingly defensive posture and they proved to the inhabitants of the occupied countries that Britain had not been defeated, thereby encouraging the first flickers of organized resistance.

They also achieved more easily recognizable results. The Hurricanes' victims included German aerial transports, German fighters which they caught by surprise when taking off, German troops whom they caught on the march, motor vehicles, petrol stores and wireless stations. And increasingly they began to attack the enemy vessels in coastal waters. One squadron which excelled at this important but dangerous work was No. 615

141

which from September to November 1941 was credited with having sunk or damaged between twenty and thirty ships. Its CO was Squadron Leader – later Wing Commander – Denys Gillam and in Douglas Bader's *Fight for the Sky* he describes the tactics used:

> We approached the target in two sections of four, each section in line abreast, alongside each other; the section leaders were in the middle of this formation of eight. At the right distance from the target, the two leaders throttled back, thus allowing the outside men to get ahead. Then all eight Hurricanes pulled up and dived on the target with cannons and machine-guns blazing. As soon as we passed over it, we were down on the water and jinking away. Out of range, we would re-form and have a second go from a different direction.
>
> The cast-iron rule was that one Hurricane or even one section of four should never attack alone. By our method, we dispersed the flak and confused the enemy gunners.

615 Squadron was often accompanied on these raids by 607 Squadron which was based at the same airfield, but its Hurricanes carried more powerful, if less accurate, weapons than cannons or machine guns – 250lb bombs. 607 Squadron in fact provides an example of another of those traits which made the Hurricane so immensely valuable. It was astonishingly versatile, particularly bearing in mind that it remained basically the same aircraft throughout its career, the different Marks of Hurricane being distinguished mainly by the different engines which powered them.

Thus Hurricanes built in Canada flew with various Packard-Merlin engines – so-called because they were produced by the Packard Motor Corporation in the United States. These machines were designated Marks X, XI, XII and XIIA, but in practice the first and last named, which carried eight machine guns, were Canadian equivalents of IIAs, while the middle pair with their twelve machine guns were Canadian IIBs.

What really made the difference between one Hurricane and another was the use to which each was put. There were a number of individual adaptations. One Mark XII, for instance, was fitted with a ski undercarriage and tail-skid for operations from snow-covered airfields. One Mark I flew as a biplane, the idea being that the extra wing would assist in providing more lift for take-offs from very small landing grounds, after which it – plus the inter-plane struts which held it in position – could be jettisoned in flight. Far more important of course were the modifications which allowed Hurricanes to fly off aircraft-carriers or be catapulted off merchantmen. And perhaps more important still was the profound change in the Hurricane's career which took place during the course of 1941.

In January of that year the RAF, as well as its 'Rhubarb' raids, commenced larger operations across the Channel, called 'Circuses'. At first these were usually carried out by Blenheim bombers, with a close escort of Hurricanes and a top cover of Spitfires. Before the year's end, however, the role of the Blenheims was being performed by the Hurricanes themselves – they, or at least a sizeable number of them, had become 'Hurribombers'.

The Hurricanes chosen to be so adapted were usually IIBs and their new weapons were two 250lb bombs under the wings. Some IICs were also equipped with bombs but these, added to the IIC's heavy 20mm cannons, lowered its performance considerably. The IIB's speed was reduced by only some 20 mph, while neither its handling characteristics nor its manoeuvrability were affected. The space needed for the bomb racks and associated wiring did mean that many IIB conversions found it beneficial to omit one machine gun on each wing, leaving the Hurribomber with ten – though some fighter-bomber squadrons preferred to keep all twelve for better protection after the bombs had been dropped.

As was hinted earlier, one of the early Hurribomber squadrons was No. 607. Among its pilots was Flight Sergeant – later Flight Lieutenant – John Brooks who relates his unit's activities in Chaz Bowyer's *Hurricane at War*:

In late 1941 the Hurricane became a fighter-bomber and its prime job was purely low-level attacks on Channel shipping and against static targets over France and the Low Countries. It was fitted with a faired bomb-rack under each wing

143

carrying (normally) two 250lb bombs. During the Dieppe raid this was doubled to two 500lb bombs – which was also the effective bomb load of the Blenheim and Boston light bombers! It was about then that skip-bombing was 'discovered' – the Americans 're-discovered' it about a year or so later, much to our amusement. At Manston (my base) one squadron [607] had bombs and 10 machine-guns (.303) and the sister squadron [615] had just four 20-mm Oerliken cannons for armament. During a shipping strike the cannons went in first to shut up the opposition and the 'bombers' used to be right in behind them. Those convoys of smallish ships used to hug the coast and were always escorted by flak ships. These were modified tugs simply bristling with guns of all sorts and could put up an awful lot of hot metal. During any attack it was necessary to fly straight at the target, just skimming the waves and releasing the bombs at the last minute. Then one had to fly straight through all the heavy flak, hoping for the best. It was now that the Hurricane was most vulnerable. Underneath the pilot was a large radiator which if it got as much as a single bullet in it usually meant 'curtains'! The engine either seized up solid or caught fire. This meant that a pilot had to get out. Unfortunately one was too low to bale out and if you did have the speed to pull up, you were a sitting duck. The casualties in such raids were very high.

Probably the most hazardous of the Hurricane's anti-shipping missions took place on 12 February 1942, on which day *Scharnhorst, Gneisenau,* the heavy cruiser *Prinz Eugen* and a suitable escort broke out of Brest to make a dash for home through the English Channel. 607 Squadron with its Hurribombers was one of the squadrons involved and Flight Sergeant Walker scored a direct hit on a flak ship with a 250lb bomb, though at the cost of his own life. 1 Squadron, flying Hurricane IICs, engaged bigger targets, raking the superstructure of three destroyers with cannon shells – though the damage done could not have been serious. Two of its aircraft did not return.

Usually Hurricane sorties were less dangerous and more

successful. On 15 May 1942, for example, the Hurribombers of 175 Squadron attacked three minesweepers, sinking two outright and damaging the third so badly that it went down later. Moreover they did not limit their attention to the Channel. They frequently crossed it, as John Brooks explains:

> Favourite targets during late 1941 and early 1942 were the German air-bases in France. The Hurricane was ideal for such work since it could fly very low (a couple of feet) and be jinked at the same time to avoid the ground defences. On a personal note, when flying the Hurricane under combat conditions I used to screw up the throttle friction nut tightly and then use both hands on the control column spade grip. This allowed one to use all one's strength in manoeuvres – although thinking back, the poor Hurricane must have been terribly strained at times.

Hurribomber sorties, which were usually protected by an escort of Spitfires, continued throughout 1942. They ranged as far south as Rheims and targets attacked successfully included not only aerodromes but road bridges, rail bridges, road vehicles, rail transport, railway stations, factories, depots, canal barges, transformer stations, troop concentrations, gun positions and distilleries.

As a culmination of the Hurricane's low-level assaults on occupied Europe, six Hurricane fighter squadrons and the Hurribombers of 174 and 175 Squadrons took part in Operation JUBILEE, the ill-fated raid on Dieppe on 19 August 1942. In the long term this would prove invaluable as it taught vital lessons which would be put to good use in the later amphibious triumphs in Sicily, Italy and eventually Normandy, but its immediate effects were less acceptable. The Canadians who made up the bulk of the attackers suffered very heavy casualties, while the RAF lost over sixty Spitfires from the fighter cover. Close support had been entrusted to the Hurricanes and twenty of them were also lost, almost all to AA fire.

In return the Hurricanes had been one of the few successes of the operation; all accounts, whether from the soldiers or from the pilots of other types, confirmed their effectiveness. Every

Hurricane squadron flew at least three missions during the day, most flew four, and among the targets bombed or strafed were gun batteries, troop positions, wireless stations, railway sidings, cranes, tanks, lorries and buildings of various kinds. It would be wearisome to give a blow-by-blow account of every sortie, but a couple of examples should suffice to represent the Hurricane's ground-attack exploits, not only at Dieppe but throughout the conflict on the Channel front.

The first Hurricane fighter squadron in action over Dieppe was No. 43, commanded by the Belgian Squadron Leader Du Vivier. It attacked buildings and gun positions close to the beaches but came under intense, accurate AA fire which provided its Hurricanes with a number of opportunities to display their incredible capacity for absorbing combat damage:

Flying Officer Turkington made a most creditable touchdown with the elevators partly missing and wholly shredded, and Pilot Officer Trenchard-Smith of Australia earned for himself the enduring name of 'Tail-less Ted' after returning to the owners a Hurricane on which the top half of the fin and the rudder had vanished and the remnants of the latter hung to the rudder post only by the bottom hinge and the control cables.

. . . The supreme exposition of all [was given by the Hurricane of Flight Lieutenant 'Freddy' Lister] . . . The panels above the cannons [on the port wing were] blown off; a four-foot square hole in the trailing edge took in the aileron up to its inboard hinge, and the outermost cannon, wrenched from its by no means slender mounting, was askew, damaging the front spar and buckling the leading edge. But the Hurricane kept flying.

. . . [On return to his base at Tangmere, Lister crash-landed at 210 mph.] Most aeroplanes of that period, hitting the ground at such speeds, would simply have disintegrated; others dug in the nose, flipped over on to their backs and crushed the skulls of their unfortunate occupants. The Hurricane, possessed of no such venomous streak, just kept going straight and level, ripping open the green turf beside

146

the runway and spewing out the brown clods to either side until, with the radiator wrenched away, it slid to a halt close to the boundary fence and the sunken road beyond. The air intake had gone, the propeller blades were all sheared at the roots, the spinner was stove in, the bottom cowlings torn. The wheel bay and cannon muzzles were packed with hard-driven earth, and the port wing was a scarcely cohesive jumble of twisted metal and torn skin. But from out of it stepped, quite unhurt though a little stunned by his good fortune, one very valuable flight commander.[1]

Lister flew three more sorties that day, by the end of which he had won a DFC. What seems in retrospect the most extraordinary part of his exploit is that it apparently never occurred to him that it might be better to bale out. He was determined to bring his 'mount' home and was justly confident that it would not fail him if he did.

The Hurribombers of 174 and 175 Squadrons also got an early start, attacking heavy gun-batteries situated on high ground behind Dieppe with 500lb bombs. 174 Squadron had taken over a number of pilots who had previously flown fighter-bombers with 607 Squadron, among them John Brooks who led a section of four on this mission – as he describes in Chaz Bowyer's *Hurricane at War*:

Some light flak came up from the gun site but it wasn't really enough to put us off. My main concern was that we would all pull out and miss the surrounding trees – this being the first time we had done formation dive-bombing at night, and with 1,000lb of bombs apiece. I went down as low as I dared to release my bombs – I couldn't really miss. I could make out the heavy guns on their white concrete bases, along with some smaller gun sites and huts. It was these smaller sites from which the guns were firing at me, so I fired back as I dived down. This was a general tactic to make the people on the ground keep their heads down . . . I pulled out at a couple of hundred feet and saw the trees loom out of the darkness in front of me. I was weaving like mad now just above the tree tops with lots of machine-gun and 40-mm stuff quite thick all around me. My bombs had 6-seconds delay fuzes, whilst the boys behind me had 2-second fuzes. This was to prevent those behind me being blown up by my bombs. Nevertheless it meant a quick and co-ordinated run over the target even with such precautions.

After what seemed a very long time I saw the whole site go up in a series of quick flashes and then felt the crump, which bounced my Hurricane about . . . We all continued to machine-gun anything that moved on the ground. By then it was light enough to see and we all had a go at some German transport which disgorged its troops in a great big hurry . . . All of our aircraft were found to have holes in them.

Undaunted by his experiences, Brooks saw further action throughout the day and would provide graphic proof of his own statement that the Hurricane 'could fly very low (a couple of feet)' by returning with a 'souvenir' in the form of the aerial of a German tank wedged in his radiator. Even so the bombs carried by the Hurricane had not really been intended for the task of smashing heavy gun emplacements, and the operation therefore prompted other Hurricane adaptations so as to provide it with still more formidable weapons for its ground-attack duties.

One such adaptation indeed had already appeared. The Hurricane IID, known as the 'tank-buster', or more rarely as the 'Hurribuster', or even affectionately as the 'tin-opener', carried two Browning .303-inch machine guns which fired tracer ammunition as an aiming aid, and two 40mm cannons. These were either Vickers Type 'S' or Rolls-Royce 'BF' – belt feed – though the former was much preferred if only because it carried a higher number of rounds per gun than did the Rolls-Royce version. Top speed, fully loaded, was 304 mph but this declined to 288 mph when the IID was fitted with a tropical filter. Most of them were, for they were mainly shipped overseas and although they had reached squadrons in the Middle East by May 1942, the only IID squadron in Britain, No. 184, did not receive its machines until the end of that year and saw no combat with them.

It would, however, see a good deal of combat when the next Hurricane variant appeared in the spring of 1943. Originally called the Mark IIE, it was at first powered by the standard Mark II Merlin XX engine, but this was later changed for a Merlin 27, whereupon the aircraft was re-designated the Mark IV, the Mark III being a proposed Packard-Merlin version which did not materialize. The Hurricane IV, like the IID, had only two machine guns but could mount almost any type of external armament. Without such encumbrances it could attain a speed of about 330 mph and had a service ceiling of 32,500 feet, but naturally its performance fell away sharply when the weapons were carried. This was really the last Hurricane version for although a very few would fly when powered by a ground-boosted Merlin 32 engine – they were known as Mark Vs – indications that this engine's life was unacceptably short soon resulted in the scheme's abandonment.

Though the Hurricane IV normally had to be escorted by Spitfires or Typhoons to protect it against hostile fighters, it was a formidable threat to any enemy on land or sea. It could carry not only 500lb bombs or 40mm cannons, but also another new and deadly weapon, as 184 Squadron's CO, Squadron Leader – later Wing Commander – Jack Rose describes in Robert Jackson's *Hawker Hurricane*:

Early in 1943 we were re-equipped with Hurricane IVs carrying a bank of four rockets under each wing. These had either 25lb armour-piercing heads or 60lb semi-armour-piercing high-explosive shells. The damage that these rockets could inflict proved to be very impressive . . . The most usual technique was to fire the rockets in a ripple, that is one pair at a time during the approach run. As there was no recoil from the rockets, there was no need to re-sight between each pair of rockets being fired, as in the case of the Vickers 'S' guns. We could, if we wished, use the Vickers guns instead of the rockets and occasionally we did so, but after a time we stuck to the RPs [rocket projectiles].

The firing range we used was Leysdown on the Isle of Sheppey . . . We were provided with an unserviceable

Churchill tank and later a Sherman too. They were transported to the Leysdown range and were set up on the beach, providing first-class durable targets. All attacks were recorded by the range officers, and my log book shows such scores as 26 and 28 out of 32 rounds fired from the Vickers guns and three or four out of eight using the 25lb AP rockets . . .

In June 1943 . . . [rocket] attacks were made on shipping off the Dutch coast. The first of these on 17 June consisted of four aircraft (we normally flew four aircraft on such operations) piloted by myself, Flight Lieutenant Ruffhead, Flying Officer Kilpatrick (Australian) and Flying Officer Cross (Canadian). We each fired our eight 60lb rockets in ripples at ships anchored close inshore and we all returned with nothing worse than a few bullet holes.

Other rocket attacks on shipping followed; nor were land targets neglected. Moreover, as was mentioned earlier, the Hurricane IV could also carry bombs or the big 40mm cannons. The first mission with the latter was mounted by 137 Squadron on 23 June 1943. The Squadron Diary, recorded in Francis K. Mason's *The Hawker Hurricane*, describes its success:

The four aircraft took off from Manston at 13:10 hours and landed safely at 15:00 hours. The Belgian coast was crossed in cloud at 1,500 feet 2 miles west of Nieuport and a goods train was attacked near Cotemark by all pilots and the engine disintegrated. Two other goods trains were found at Statiestrate. F/L Bryan and F/O Chalmers attacked one, seeing strikes and leaving it covered in dirty black smoke. P/O Brunet and F/O Davidson dealt with the other, resulting in its engine's disintegration with the boiler knocked off the bogies. Intense light flak was experienced here. Near Lightervelde P/O Brunet and F/O Chalmers shot up a large army lorry. At Thielt a small train was attacked by all pilots and left emitting smoke. Two barges were cannoned next and badly damaged and the four aircraft returned to Manston.

Hurricane IVs armed with various weapons continued to engage targets, either as opportunity offered or as specifically selected, throughout 1943. On 2 September, for instance, 137 and 164 Squadrons, escorted by Typhoons, delivered rocket strikes against lock gates on the Dutch Hansweert Canal. Airfields were also targeted, and during December and the early months of 1944, attention was particularly directed onto 'No-balls' – this being the code name for the V1 launching sites along the French coast. Since the Germans hoped that their secret weapons might yet turn the tide of war, the sites were protected by innumerable AA batteries, and casualties among the attacking aircraft were very high. The Free French ace Pierre Clostermann was flying one of the escorting Spitfires when 184 Squadron attacked a 'No-ball' on 20 December. In his book *The Big Show*, he paints a terrifying portrait of the dangers that 184 Squadron's pilots had to face:

The Hurricanes began their dive, slap into the machine-gun bullets. The tracer bullets formed a wall of steel and explosive round the target.

The inevitable happened. Powerless I watched the tragedy. Flight Lieutenant Roughhead,[2] just as he let go his salvo of rockets, was hit and killed instantly. His disabled Hurricane recovered with incredible violence and zoomed vertically upwards, its propeller stationery. At the top of the trajectory one wing wilted, the aircraft hung as on a thread suspended in space, motionless, then went into a spin.

As in a nightmare I saw Warrant Officer Pearce's Hurricane literally mown down by a burst of 37-mm. The tail came off, the machine crashed into a wood, scything down the trees, scattering jets of burning petrol.

The other two Hurricanes attacked simultaneously. Struck by a direct hit, Sergeant Clive's machine exploded and was soon nothing but an inchoate mass of flame, dragging a long trail of black smoke.

By a miracle, Bush the Australian was luckier; he succeeded not only in planting his eight rockets in the control room but even in extricating himself from the barrage of flak, in spite of an enormous gash in his fuselage, not to mention two bullets in the thigh and one in the side.

Such sacrifices were not in vain. The campaign against the V1 sites did not prevent their being used against Britain, but it did delay their appearance until after D-Day, during the build-up for which southern England would have presented an exceptionally vulnerable target. When they did arrive, the flying bombs caused considerable damage, both moral and material, but they never looked like reversing the tide of war; indeed by early September their launching sites had been overrun by the triumphant Allied armies. The Hurricanes had played only a small part in the postponement of the V1 bombardment, but not an unworthy one as Jack Rose proudly tells us:

I can remember seeing an Intelligence report at about this time in which damage to the 'No-ball' sites was given in relation to the weight of bombs dropped by various types of aircraft. The catagories were heavy bombers, medium bombers, and rocket-firing aircraft. Although we had loads of only 480lb (8 x 60lb) the damage inflicted by our attacks per ton of 'bombs' dropped was, I suppose understandably, very much greater than the damage per ton dropped by the – mostly American – medium and heavy bombers.

Prior to the D-Day landings the Hurricane IV squadrons were re-equipped with Typhoons, the successes of which, especially in Normandy, owed much to the experiences of their predecessors. In fact all the Hurricanes based in Britain had by then been relegated from front-line to supporting duties. These included training, meteorological flights and air-sea rescue support, while a Polish squadron, No. 309, continued to fly Hurricane IICs on shipping protection patrols off the east coast of Scotland until October 1944.

Yet even so Hurricanes did take part in the great invasion, for on 6 June 63 Squadron's IICs would be found ranging above the beaches rectifying one of the weaknesses revealed at Dieppe by spotting fall of shot for the bombarding naval units. During the

Normandy campaign also, Hurricanes continued their secondary tasks, to which they added that of carrying high-priority despatches to and from the Continent. On 10 June two such unarmed IICs landed on an airfield which turned out to be still in German hands. They took off again in some haste, but successfully. No one after all could have imagined either the Hurricane or its pilots being left completely out of the fighting.

NOTES
1 James Beedle: *43 Squadron: Royal Flying Corps; Royal Air Force. The History of the Fighting Cocks 1916–1966.* His account of this episode is based on the stories of those involved, and also his own recollections, for he was at this time a sergeant serving with 43 Squadron as an engine fitter and he witnessed the return of the battered Hurricanes to Tangmere.
2 This is a misnomer. Flight Lieutenant 'Roughhead' was in fact the Flight Lieutenant Ruffhead who had taken part in 184 Squadron's first anti-shipping strike, described earlier. Apart from Jack Rose, all the pilots who had flown on that mission were killed during later rocket attacks – which emphasizes still further how perilous these were.

Chapter 12

Decision in the Desert

In the Mediterranean theatre the Hurricane stayed in front-line service until the end of hostilities. Its greatest services, however, were undoubtedly performed from late 1941 to mid–1943, during which time the struggle for North Africa swung backwards and forwards in a series of bewildering changes of fortune.

During the latter part of 1941, the Allied land forces were expanded into the Eighth Army, and the supporting air arm into the Western Desert Air Force – officially; in practice the word 'Western' was rarely used. On 18 November both commenced a massive offensive, code-named Operation CRUSADER. This ultimately raised the siege of Tobruk and forced Rommel's retirement to the bottleneck of El Agheila on the western border of Cyrenaica, which he had reached by 6 January 1942.

General Auchinleck, the Allied C-in-C, Middle East, was confident that Eighth Army would soon resume its progress towards Libya's capital, Tripoli, but this was not to be. By this time Kesselring had begun his assault on Malta, under cover of which Axis convoys were at last able to reach North Africa. On 21 January it was the enemy land forces, now rechristened *Panzerarmee Afrika*, which took the offensive.

As already mentioned, Auchinleck never did appreciate the importance of Malta, so was taken completely by surprise. Moreover he persisted in the delusion that he could control the fast-moving Desert campaigns from a distance through the medium of his former Deputy Chief of Staff, Major General Neil Ritchie, whom he had appointed to command Eighth Army. On this loyal but luckless officer Auchinleck showered 'advice' which it was difficult to regard as other than orders, and on him also Auchinleck would later try to lay the blame for subsequent misfortunes.

There would certainly be plenty of these. By 5 February Rommel had been halted at Gazala, west of Tobruk, but among his conquests had been the vital Martuba airfield complex, the loss of which tightened the Axis grip on Malta. Then on 26 May Rommel resumed his advance, drove Eighth Army out of the Gazala Line and completed his victory on 21 June with the capture of Tobruk.

Through all the changes of fortune, Hurricanes were in constant action, though often operating from unsuitable landing grounds and occasionally having to evacuate them at very short notice on the approach of enemy columns. They performed reconnaissance duties, they dropped supply canisters to isolated positions, they delivered top secret messages, and of course they dealt with raids by enemy bombers and acted as escorts for Allied ones. The Canadian Flight Lieutenant – later Wing Commander – George Keefer flew Hurricanes with 274 Squadron at this time; in *Fighters Over the Desert* by Christopher Shores and Hans Ring, he comments that:

Regarding the aircraft we flew, I guess I felt as most Hurricane pilots felt, that they were more than a match for the Italian aircraft, ie CR 42s, Fiat G 50s, Macchi 200s and Macchi 202s.[1] On the other hand, in many respects, they were not equal to the 109s used by the Germans. I cannot think of one occasion when we encountered 109s and were above them. They were invariably on top of us every time we met. They seemed to be faster, had a better climb and much better altitude performance. Notwithstanding all this, the old 'Hurri' provided some considerable comfort in its ruggedness and extreme manoeuvrability. I certainly had the feeling that with this ruggedness and manoeuvrability no one could get me as long as I could see him coming.

Moreover, if they sometimes suffered heavy losses when 'bounced' from above by 109s, the Hurricanes rarely failed to engage the more important enemy bombers successfully. As a result Eighth Army's retreats never degenerated into routs. When its divisions holding the Gazala Line fell back to avoid being cut off, the coastal road was jammed with lorries bunched helplessly together. Yet during this retreat only six Allied soldiers died as a result of attacks by enemy aeroplanes.

It was just prior to this retirement – and possibly the reason for its successful accomplishment – that perhaps the most desperate air battle of the Desert campaigns took place. On 12 June 1942 four squadrons of Hurricanes met a huge formation of Junkers Ju 87s and Ju 88s, guarded by 109s and Macchi MC 202s. 33 Squadron was the unlucky one, losing three aircraft and two pilots, though it damaged five enemy fighters. 213 Squadron did better, shooting down two 109s for the loss of two Hurricanes, the pilot of one of which baled out, and 274 Squadron better still, downing four 109s without loss. While the fighter escort was thus engaged the Hurricanes of 73 Squadron tackled the bombers, destroying five Stukas, plus one Ju 88, damaging four more Stukas and all returning safely to base.

Of 274 Squadron's victims, two fell to Sergeant James Dodds who would eventually be credited with the destruction of fourteen enemy aircraft. Among these were ten 109s or MC 202s which had performances superior to that of his Hurricane – on paper at any rate. He gained his last victories – a pair of MC 202s – on 17 June 1942. Thereafter most of his operations, like those of 274 Squadron's other pilots, consisted of strikes against Axis vehicles with 250lb bombs.

274 Squadron was neither the only nor the first Hurribomber squadron in the Desert. As early as 20 November 1941 during Operation CRUSADER the old Hurricane Is of 80 Squadron were armed with four 40lb bombs under each wing. These inflicted considerable damage on enemy lorries and even caused casualties among tank crews who were decapitated when they opened their hatches to see what was happening, or blown to pieces when caught by surprise outside their vehicles.

Nor did these fighter-bomber Hurricanes neglect the 'fighter' part of their title. On 8 December 1941, 80 squadron not only left the coastal road strewn with blazing transports over almost a mile, but beat off an attack by 109s, downing two of them. Next day their CO, Squadron Leader Michael Stephens, while leading another Hurribomber raid, was engaged by a Macchi MC 202. Wounded in both feet, with his Hurricane on fire, Stephens still shot down his attacker before baling out, beating out his burning clothes during his descent. He recovered from his injuries to be awarded a DSO.

Hurricane strikes were also made against Axis aircraft on the ground. 33 Squadron delivered three strafing raids on the airfield at Agedabia in the first eight days of December, destroying or damaging at least thirty enemy warplanes, including a CR 42 which Sergeant Challis hit with his Hurricane's wingtip in a really low-level attack. When the Allies advanced to El Agheila they found 458 wrecked Axis aeroplanes on the Cyrenaican landing grounds, plus many more in various resting places in the desert. A large proportion of these bore the scars inflicted by the bombs, cannon shells or machine-gun bullets of Hawker Hurricanes.

Ground attacks were delivered throughout the North African campaign by Allied airmen in general and the Hurricane pilots in particular. In *Fighters Over the Desert*, Messrs Shores and Ring include a tribute to their activities from an unusual source. The German 'ace' Werner Schroer, at that time an Oberleutnant (Lieutenant) flying 109s, admits, with commendable honesty, that:

I believe we made some mistakes; like the RAF we should have concentrated on attacks on vehicles, tanks, forces, airfields, etc., but we shirked this as often as possible. I remember well the devastating effect on morale of such attacks on our forces. During the few ground attacks which I flew, the English soldiers lay on their backs and shot at us with their rifles. To the contrary, what did our men do? Out of their trucks, running away for cover – maybe it was the result of the constant British air attacks.

It was indeed – and on 8 June 1942 an entirely new form of attack was introduced by 6 Squadron. The importance of this unit may be seen from the fact that its CO was a Wing Commander, Roger Porteous (who, alas, was to be killed flying a jet aircraft after the war). His second in command was the South African Squadron Leader Weston-Burt, and in Chaz Bowyer's *Hurricane at War* he tells us all about the Squadron's new equipment:

> The Hurricane IID was, at that time, a secret weapon. It was in fact a Hurricane II fitted with two Vickers 'S' guns of 40-mm calibre, slung one under each wing, and two .303 inch machine-guns. It was created for the prime role of tank destruction from the air . . . [and the 'S' guns' shells] were armour piercing and designed to break up into fragments on emerging inside the tank, so as to achieve as much damage as possible to the tank's intestines and the crew . . . The rounds could be fired in a burst but this so depressed the nose that in practice they were fired in single pairs, bringing the gunsight back on to target for each pair. It took not much more than half a second to get each pair away.
> . . . [When engaging tanks] the run-in [was made] at about 20–40 feet above the ground. Opening with the first pair [of shells] at about 1,000 yards, two more pairs could be got away accurately before breaking off the attack. It is no exaggeration to say that any good pilot would guarantee to hit his target with one or more pairs on each attack.

6 Squadron's first strike on 8 June destroyed four tanks and three half-tracked troop-carriers among other vehicles. Exactly a week later its 'bag' was five tanks, five lorries and an anti-tank gun. In the course of this action Flight Lieutenant Hillier struck a tank, knocking off his Hurricane's tailwheel and the bottom half of the rudder – damage which did not prevent him from getting his aircraft back to base.

Sadly, when the Axis army delivered its assault on Tobruk, the Desert Air Force had already been driven from its forward landing grounds. Kesselring, at the cost of abandoning sustained raids on Malta, had sent large reinforcements to North Africa, and he now

158

hurled every Stuka he could find against Tobruk's defences to clear the way for the attackers. German accounts leave no doubt as to the reason for the dive-bombers' effectiveness: they 'had no "Huren-kähne" to harass them'.

Yet at this moment of greatest success, Rommel made a fatal mistake. It had been intended that once Tobruk had fallen he would pause on the Egyptian frontier while his communications were guaranteed by the conquest of Malta. Now, intoxicated by his triumph and the award of a field marshal's baton, and heedless of the protests of Kesselring, Rommel won the consent of that other great gambler, Hitler, to dash for the Suez Canal, leaving Malta still unsubdued behind him.

He could not have reached a more catastrophic decision. Every mile he advanced into Egypt his supply line became more perilous and his Italian troops fell further behind the Germans – as did his air forces, the bulk of which had in any case been compelled to leave for Sicily to counter renewed threats from Malta. And all this at a time when Eighth Army, which even after the fall of Tobruk contained many more men, tanks, guns and supplies than *Panzerarmee Afrika*, was receiving massive reinforcements. There can be little doubt that a resolute stand at Mersa Matruh would have stopped Rommel in his tracks, but unfortunately Auchinleck, now in personal command of Eighth Army, had decided to fight a delaying action only before falling back to El Alamein.

Here Rommel's route lay through a 40-mile gap between the Mediterranean and the huge, impassable quicksand known as the Qattara Depression. Furthermore lack of petrol meant that when he attacked on 1 July he could do so only in the north, where the Allied defences were at their strongest, having originally been ordered by Wavell. He commanded just 1,500 exhausted motorized infantrymen and fifty-five tanks, which, contrary to oft-repeated myth, were inferior to the British armour in quality as well as quantity. Not surprisingly his advance ground to a halt.

Rommel had just one card left to play. By 3 July his airmen had caught up with him and he flung his Stukas against El Alamein in the hope that they might shatter the defences as they had done at Tobruk. This time though they were met by Hurricanes, particularly Major Le Mesurier's No. 1 Squadron, South African Air

Force. While 274 Squadron kept the escorting 109s occupied, the South Africans tore into the dive-bombers, claiming thirteen destroyed, nine of them above the heads of the delighted soldiers of Eighth Army.

Now Auchinleck took the offensive, urging his men to 'destroy the enemy as far east as possible'. There would never be a better opportunity for doing just that. Eighth Army had a short, easily defended supply line; Rommel a long, tenuous one. Eighth Army had gained still more reinforcements and its strength in tanks increased to over 200 by 10 July, almost 400 by the 20th; the number of German tanks varied from under thirty to about fifty. Eighth Army could call on a dominant air force; the Axis shortages were such that even at this late date the Hurricanes encountered biplane CR 42s – a fact affording much satisfaction to 1 Squadron SAAF which shot down five of them on 13 July.

Yet despite these immense advantages, Auchinleck failed utterly to destroy or even drive back his enemy. His forces were not concentrated, there was no co-ordination between the different arms, and the British tanks were dashed uselessly against German artillery. These were all mistakes which had been made in the past but had still not been rectified, and to them Auchinleck had added a new one: a failure to make use of his air arm, probably because he had moved his Headquarters well inland, miles away from that of the Desert Air Force.

In early August it was *Panzerarmee Afrika* which received reinforcements. These brought its strength nearer to an even balance with Eighth Army than ever before and included new tanks that were at last really superior to any the British had in North Africa, then or later. Thus encouraged, Rommel planned a new offensive which would become known as the Battle of Alam Halfa. Happily, before it was fought, Churchill and the Chief of the Imperial General Staff, General Sir Alan Brooke, visited Egypt and drastic changes were made.

As C-in-C, Middle East, Churchill and Brooke appointed General Sir Harold Alexander, who had already shown cool leadership in times of crisis at Dunkirk and in Burma, while the dynamic, if controversial, Lieutenant General Bernard Montgomery took over Eighth Army. That he revived its shattered morale is well known, but it is often not appreciated that he also dramatically altered existing plans for the coming battle – reversing the mania for dispersal, bringing up soldiers previously employed guarding the cities of Egypt, strengthening minefields and refusing to fight the mobile action which Auchinleck had intended (and at which the Germans excelled); instead placing his tanks in prepared defensive positions, backed by anti-tank guns.

He also re-established Eighth Army's Headquarters alongside that of the Desert Air Force – and this was no token gesture as the Royal Air Force Official History[2] gracefully acknowledges:

> Beyond this, however, he [Montgomery] also brought to his post a remarkably keen, clear and vigorous appreciation of the part that could and should be played by air forces in a land battle. Commanders like Auchinleck and Ritchie had never been anything but highly co-operative; but Montgomery insisted that goodwill was translated at all stages into practical action. If air co-operation was the gospel in the GOC's caravan, it would also be the gospel all the way from base to front line.

Co-operation in action would prove decisive in the Battle of Alam Halfa. It opened on the night of 30 August with attacks by Junkers Ju 88s on Allied landing grounds. They were met by the Hurricanes of 73 Squadron which was now operating mainly as a night-fighter unit, and lost two of their number to Squadron Leader Johnston and Warrant Officer Joyce.

Thereafter although the Hurricanes sometimes suffered when 'bounced' by 109s, they dispersed formations of Junkers Ju 87s or Ju 88s during daylight hours as well, 127 and 274 Squadrons shooting down six Stukas in one encounter on 2 September. About 375 Axis soft-skinned vehicles were also destroyed in the course of the battle, a large proportion by Hurribombers. 7 Squadron SAAF added a new twist on 4 September, making a highly effective attack with 'sticky bombs' which would not glance off the sides of tanks, an attack delivered at such low level that two Hurricanes had to force-land, having been damaged by splinters from their own weapons.

By that time Rommel was already falling back. The danger to Cairo and Alexandria was removed for ever and Eighth Army and Desert Air Force could make ready for the fresh offensive which they knew must follow. For this Montgomery was able to build up his strength, especially in tanks, well beyond that of his opponent, but *Panzerarmee Afrika* did have one immense advantage. It was protected by half-a-million mines together with every form of booby trap that human ingenuity could devise. Behind this sinister barrier it could hope to take fearful toll of any number of attackers.

Fifteen Hurricane squadrons were among the aerial forces supporting Eighth Army. No. 6, as Squadron Leader Weston-Burt recalls for us, was very quickly in action:

> The battle of El Alamein was heralded at 1100 hours on the night of October 23rd, 1942 by the largest artillery barrage the world had ever known. From our airfields we could see the whole western horizon lit by thousands of gun flashes. The following morning I was sent off with six Hurricane IIDs on a target of 15 tanks and two half-tracks. We found them, attacked and did considerable damage. I personally claimed three tanks definitely hit.

7 Squadron SAAF had now also been re-equipped with Hurricane IIDs, 80 and 274 Squadrons flew Hurribombers, and 208 and 40 Squadron SAAF took care of reconnaissance missions. The following squadrons all flew Hurricanes on fighter duties: 33, 94, 127, 213, 238, a squadron with Greek personnel, 335, a Canadian unit, 417, and 1 Squadron SAAF. Yet the first Hurricane squadron to take part in the battle was No. 73, and as early as the night on which it opened. One of its pilots was Sergeant David Green, who would later rise to the rank of group captain. In *The Desert Air War 1939–1945* by Richard Townshend Bickers, he explains how:

> Offensive sorties [at night] were of two types, recce/ground attack and intruders. Both were flown by single aircraft. On recce/ground attack, we might be given a specific area where

targets could be expected, either through intelligence reports or observations by the day squadrons. If the latter were the source, we were given a more general area or line, such as the coastal road, along which to seek out targets of any sort, opportunity targets. It was entirely up to each pilot to decide how and when to attack . . . [Enemy airfields were the targets of intruder missions and in either case] if there was a moon or any other sort of lighter sector, such as dawn or dusk, the attack was always made from the darker sector. The approach had to be steady, in a 25- to 30-degree dive. Fire was usually opened at about 1,000 ft and continued to a bottom limit of about 500 ft. On breaking away, a climbing turn was made immediately, back towards the dark sector. It was, however, a very hit and miss affair particularly where the height was concerned. There were times when, with the altimeter still reading a respectable altitude, I have suddenly become aware of vehicles, tents etc immediately beneath the belly of the aircraft. One wonders who was the more surprised, oneself or the enemy.

It will doubtless cause no surprise to say that the Hurricanes justified all that could have been hoped of them. They broke up enemy air raids, 213 Squadron and 1 Squadron SAAF for instance downing six Stukas without loss on 2 November. Next day 127 Squadron did suffer losses, being attacked from above by 109s which shot down six of its aircraft. Yet even this was not wholly disastrous, for while the German fighters were thus engaged, another Hurricane squadron, No. 80, attacked the Stukas they were supposed to be escorting; enemy records confirm that nine of these failed to return.

The Hurricanes' actions against enemy ground forces show few such individual successes but their total achievement is impressive enough: the destruction of 39 tanks, 42 guns, 212 lorries or troop carriers, 26 petrol bowsers, over 200 other forms of transport and 4 small ammunition or fuel dumps. Thirty-seven Hurricanes and twenty-five Hurricane pilots were lost.

Nor did the Hurricanes' activities cease when on 4 November *Panzerarmee Afrika*, for the first time in the Desert War, fell back, not in good order but in full flight. On 13 November a Hurricane Wing consisting of Squadron Leader Olver's 213 Squadron and 238 Squadron under Squadron Leader Marples, flew to Landing Ground 125, about 140 miles behind enemy lines. 213 Squadron's personnel included Flying Officer Albert Houle who was then an acting flight commander and who would also in due course become a group captain. In *Fight for the Sky: True Stories of Wartime Fighter Pilots* by Bruce Barrymore Halpenny, Houle summarizes the progress of a mission with the innocent code name of Operation CHOCOLATE:

Immediately after lunch Wingco Darwin gathered us around him for a briefing for the first show. He told us that sections were going out on divergent vectors to hit the [coastal] road at seven points from El Agheila to Benghazi. We marked our own positions on the map and drew vectors and distances to various points on this road. These had to be memorized as we were not allowed to carry the maps. Our R/T switch was not to be turned on and under no circumstances was it to be used, even if it was a case of life or death. After strafing we were to keep down low so that Jerry couldn't plot our line of flight and thus find the landing ground. My section included Flying Officer Roy McKay, Flight Sergeant Harry Compton from Canada and Pilot Officer Gordie Carrick from Australia. Our striking point was about 10 miles north of Agedabia. We were then to swing north until out of ammunition and return. I had primed the boys to waste no time after the briefing so that we could get off first. It worked and we roared away to draw first blood . . .

After an hour of flying right on the deck the country got a little greener. Then we could see transports, bags of them in the distance, rolling for safety behind the El Agheila line. We hit the road and turned north, weaving across from side to side, taking shots at any target that presented itself. As soon as we had knocked out a few vehicles there was a pile-up behind. That gave us a field day. We attacked big six-wheelers absolutely jammed with troops, packed so tight that only a few could extricate themselves and jump clear before cannon bullets started tearing into the mass. Then McKay and I spotted a Fieseler Storch stooging down the road towards us. We both went for it . . . When the Storch saw one or both of us, it did a violent turn to port, stalled, spun and went straight in . . . I don't think that either of us had hit it. It burst into flames on hitting the deck from a height of about 200 ft. Both of us went back to shooting up the defenceless trucks and armoured cars. There was no return fire so we had little to worry about. When all our guns were empty we turned for home and found it without much trouble. As we were the first section back the groundcrews were all waiting to hear how we made out. When we told them about the pickings, they went wild with delight . . .

The other sections came back one by one with exactly the same story. The venture was a howling success, although we had lost [Pilot Officers] Bart Campbell and Gordie Waite [the Wing's only losses in this operation] . . . Friday the 13th was an unlucky day for a good many of the enemy.

A spirit of comradeship prevailed that night. Fires were hidden as well as possible, and a guard was mounted in case of a surprise attack. We put our beds up in the open and slept like children. The next morning the C.O. [of 213 Squadron, Squadron Leader Olver] took twelve aircraft to attack the aerodrome at Agedabia. I was left out of this show . . .

[Shortly after dawn on 15 November] Wingco Darwin led six of us off on a strafe of Gialo, sometimes spelled Jalo, an airport about 100 miles to the south-west. We had gone about 40 miles when Darwin spotted a dust cloud and went over to investigate. We were using the R/T sparingly by this time. Suddenly it came to life with 'Prang them boys. They're Heinies.' We went to work. There were eight armoured cars . . . and after ten minutes . . . they were completely destroyed. One group made for a hill to set up a machine gun, but one of the boys blew it and most of its would-be gunners up. Other dust clouds could be seen farther along the trail. We hit back for base to rearm and refuel. The Wingco laid on aircraft from both squadrons to go out in relays of six and get everything on that back trail.

165

He also ordered me to lead a formation of six to complete our interrupted visit to Gialo.

We took off and after about 40 miles hit the real Sahara Desert; giant cones of sand possibly 200 ft in height stretched as far as the eye could see. It was a forsaken land, a bad place to have engine trouble. We only passed over a corner of the Sahara and struck level country beyond. Finding the Gialo Oasis was not hard and I was right over the landing ground before I realized it. We certainly weren't expected. Mechanics continued to work on the aircraft as we attacked. When we were finished six burning wrecks was all that was left of a few Cant 1007s, Savoia 79s and a Ju 88 . . . The surrounding desert was literally covered with dispersed armoured cars. We did target practice until out of ammunition . . .

On the morning of the 16th, we gave Gialo another working over, packed up and left immediately. Jerry had despatched a force to seek us out but the birds had flown . . . A rough estimate showed 125 lorries and armoured cars had been destroyed (flamers), over 250 had been damaged or destroyed and ten aircraft had been destroyed on the ground and two in the air.[3] . . . We will never know how many troops were killed during the strafing attacks on the packed transport vehicles. The German retreat was certainly delayed and their digging in behind the El Agheila line must have been disrupted also. It was a show that few of us will forget.

Such activities ensured that this time the Allied advance did not lose its momentum. The Martuba airfields were recaptured just in time to secure the safe passage of a convoy which reached Malta on the night of 19–20 November, finally raising the siege of the island. El Agheila had fallen by 17 December.

Meanwhile on 8 December 73 Squadron had encountered a formation of Junkers Ju 88s attempting to bomb an Allied convoy heading for Benghazi. The Hurricanes promptly engaged them and in *The Desert Air War 1939–1945* by Richard Townshend Bickers, Pilot Officer – later Squadron Leader – Maurice Smyth describes a routine encounter that had a special significance for 73 Squadron:

This boy did a turn to starboard through the cloud – he was about a mile from me – and the cloud was about 600 ft thick. I estimated where he would come out the other side, set course accordingly and kept my height. I turned and dived where I assumed he'd come out, and got him. He was only about four or five hundred yards away, turning into the convoy. For once I had height on a German aircraft and was catching him. At 400 yds I got pinpoint harmonization on my cannons, so took very careful aim and hit him across the back of the crew's quarters and the starboard engine. The engine appeared to go right out. By this time he was turning inside me, so I had to break away to starboard and when I reversed my turn again he had disappeared, except that there was a boiling cloud of water in the sea.[4] This was the squadron's three hundredth victory.

On 23 January 1943, three months to the day since the start of the Battle of El Alamein, Eighth Army ended a 1,400-mile advance with the capture of Tripoli. For the soldiers it was a day of supreme elation but their commander, when congratulating his men, did not forget those who had shared in their triumph:

On your behalf I have sent a special message to the Allied Air Forces that have co-operated with us. I don't suppose that any army has ever been supported by such a magnificent air striking force. I have always maintained that the Eighth Army and the RAF in the Western Desert together constitute one fighting machine, and therein lies our great strength.

At least comparable support was, however, already being given to other Allied soldiers elsewhere in North Africa. In the early hours of 8 November 1942, the Hurricanes of 43 Squadron left Gibraltar for Maison Blanche aerodrome near Algiers. It was a mission fraught with anxiety for if the airfield proved to be in hostile hands the Hurricanes would have nowhere to land, while even with their long-range tanks, they would not have had enough fuel to return to Gibraltar.

Mercifully, when they reached Maison Blanche the airfield was held by American troops, part of the forces successfully committed to Operation TORCH, the Allied landings in Vichy French North Africa. The Hurricanes of 253 Squadron were next to arrive, forming a Wing with No. 43, and both units soon proved especially valuable since they were the only fighters with sufficient range to cover a new Allied landing at Bougie, 120 miles east of Algiers. Their leader, Wing Commander – later Group Captain – Pedley, relates a particularly successful mission in *Fighters Over Tunisia* by Christopher Shores, Hans Ring and William N. Hess:

> On the evening of 13 November, I personally took off for the third time that day and flew towards Bougie . . . When I got to Bougie . . . I was horrified to discover that several ships were on fire, including a large transport. It was practically dark, but searching around in the gloom I suddenly saw a Ju 88 diving down from above, presumably being unable to see my Hurricane against the black background of the sea. At close range I opened fire, nearly head-on, and immediately after passing me the e/a blew up and fell in three flaming pieces into the water. This certainly convinced me that providing the Hurricane IIC could be brought within range of its quarry the firepower of its four 20-mm cannons was devastating.
>
> I circled the scene of the crash and then flew to the north of the shipping only to be confronted at once by a line of Savoia Marchetti torpedo-bombers approaching from seaward. Turning in behind them, I picked out one aircraft a bit apart from the rest and opened fire on it, at a distance. After several sustained bursts the e/a wobbled and then struck the water. By now it was dark, I had lost sight of the other bombers, and the anti-aircraft fire was intense; being at the limits of my fuel reserve I then turned away for base.

But while Allied forces were securing Algeria, Hitler was pouring men into Tunisia, and in early December the weather broke, turning Allied communications into a sea of mud. This wrecked the chances of a successful Allied invasion of Tunisia from the west. The task had therefore to be left to Eighth Army, moving forward from Tripoli – and across its path lay the formidable defences of the Mareth Line.

These had originally been designed to protect the French from the Italians; now ironically they protected Germans and Italians from the British – and from the French, for a Free French force under General Leclerc had joined Eighth Army after coming all the way across the Sahara from French Equatorial Africa. It was now pushed forward to Ksar Rhilane to screen an outflanking movement round the Mareth Line, which Montgomery hoped would divert the defenders' attention from his main offensive directly against it.

Unfortunately the Germans discovered Leclerc's men and on 10 March 1943, a strong enemy column, containing tanks, half-tracks, armoured cars and supply lorries, set out to destroy them. The Eighth Army in turn looked to the RAF for assistance and it was 6 Squadron's Hurricane tank-busters which answered the call. Squadron Leader Weston-Burt had taken over command of 6 Squadron by this time, and in Chaz Bowyer's *Hurricane at War*, he tells us how:

We took off, 13 of us for the first attack, leaving six in reserve . . .

At the position where the [enemy] column was reported to be I looked down and, with considerable surprise, saw them almost immediately beneath us. We were not in a good position to attack. We liked to espy our target from some distance, dive and come in at very low level hoping to achieve some measure of surprise. As we had been seen I decided to go straight down into the attack, and in so doing received a large shell in my port wing. I did not know until then that in diving straight at a gun firing towards one, one could see the shells coming up. For some five minutes we flew to and fro across the column, dealing out savage destruction. Each time a tank went on fire there were shouts of exultation over the R/T. When I thought we must have knocked out every tank and vehicle, and having seen none of our aircraft go down, I thought I would not push our luck too far and called the squadron together and headed for home . . . The Group Captain [Group Captain Atcherley] no doubt hearing it all over the R/T, despatched the remaining six IIDs under my senior Flight Commander, Flight Lieutenant Bluett, to give the 'coup de grace'. On arrival at base, Sorman, I resisted the impulse to do a low victory roll to indicate to those on the ground the success of our mission. It was as well that I did, because after landing I found I had a nine inch hole in the ten inch main spar of my left wing! . . . The Germans sent out tank recovery vehicles and removed some of the tanks but a ground reconnaissance proved that our claims of almost complete destruction of the column were no exaggeration.

The main assault on the Mareth Line proved much less satisfactory, but Montgomery, often blandly described as a cautious, unimaginative general, reacted with superb flexibility, transferring his main weight to the subsidiary outflanking movement – the famous 'left hook'. Once more he received invaluable aid from the squadrons of the RAF, including 6 Squadron which destroyed or damaged thirty-two tanks during the battle, while the Hurribombers of 241 Squadron, based in Algeria, flew south on 23 March to assist with attacks on gun positions, lorries and petrol vehicles. By the evening of 27 March the Axis troops were pouring back from the Mareth Line to avoid being cut off, and their total defeat was then certain. It was concluded on 13 May when all their forces in North Africa surrendered.

The end of the fighting in North Africa also marked the end of the Hurricane as a major participant in the Mediterranean air war, though individual squadrons remained in action for two years longer. They performed defensive duties such as providing cover for Allied convoys, but they were mainly engaged on intruder missions against targets on the ground or at sea. On 23 July 1943 for instance, a second Greek Hurricane squadron, No. 336, saw action for the first time when it attacked enemy installations in Crete for the loss of two pilots. Earlier on the night of 9 July, 73 Squadron, now based in Malta, had found yet another new task: ranging over Sicily to knock out the searchlights which might have located the gliders or towing aircraft that were carrying out the preliminary airborne invasion of the island.

In February 1944, 6 Squadron, which had re-equipped with rocket-firing Hurricane IVs, moved to Grottaglie in southern Italy. From then until July it engaged a number of targets on land but even more at sea, being credited with having sunk or damaged over fifty vessels, including freighters, schooners, barges, ferries, landing-craft, dredgers and tugs.

As the Germans retired from the Balkans in the autumn of 1944, 6 Squadron sent detachments to Greece and to the Adriatic island of Vis, from which they could participate in the fighting in Yugoslavia, and where they were joined by 351, a squadron of Yugoslav airmen also flying rocket-firing Hurricane IVs. On 1 December 1944 6 Squadron destroyed a Tiger tank – the Germans' largest, carrying an 88mm gun – and badly damaged two others. Next day it wrecked a further tank and two mobile guns. During December 351 Squadron claimed twelve motor vehicles, a power station, a wireless station and a command post.

In February 1945 both 6 and 351 Squadrons moved to Prkos in Yugoslavia, from which they continued to attack transports on land and on the water. Their campaign was now to reach a perfect culmination. On 1 May, just a week before the surrender of Germany, 6 Squadron flew its last mission over the Gulf of Trieste. When the Hurricanes appeared, twenty-five vessels of different types, sixteen of them troopships, hoisted white flags. It was a fitting personal capitulation to the aircraft which had been the most important Allied fighter during the early years of the war in Europe, and was still striking at its country's foes when that war ended.

NOTES

1 This was perhaps overgenerous. The Macchi MC 202 was a very good fighter which possessed a top speed of 370 mph and was highly manoeuvrable, though it did carry an armament of only two 12.7mm and two 7.7mm machine guns.
2 Volume II, appropriately entitled: *The Fight Avails*.
3 This estimate did inevitably exaggerate the enemy's losses somewhat. Probably a grand total of 300 or so vehicles were destroyed or crippled. On the other hand it appears that fifteen enemy aircraft were at least

disabled on the ground. The two destroyed in the air were the Fieseler Storch mentioned in Houle's account (which was officially credited to McKay), and a Savoia Marchetti SM 79 shot down on 14 November by Flight Lieutenant Neil Cameron of 213 Squadron – later Air Chief Marshal Sir Neil Cameron, Chief of the Air Staff.

4 Observers on the convoy confirmed that the Ju 88 had crashed, one of the crew being picked up by a rescue ship.

Chapter 13

Last Lap

The Japanese, with suicidal courage, fought on. Although their spate of conquests had ended by mid-1942, their airmen remained on the offensive for a time, not least on the India–Burma frontier, and Hurricanes continued to oppose them, in the process operating from an unusual base, as the RAF Official History points out:[1]

> Bounding one side of that great open space, the Maidan of Calcutta, runs a red-coloured road, fifty yards wide as measured between the balustrades enclosing it. At the far end, a white marble building, erected to commemorate an empress already half-forgotten, gleams and winks in the sultry sunshine, and about half-way along it calm-faced Lord Lansdowne and inscrutable Lord Roberts, graven in stone, look down benignly from their pedestals. In the summer, autumn and winter of 1942, the statues of the pro-consul and his military colleague were the mute witnesses of a new and striking use for this impressive highway. It had become the main landing ground for the Hurricanes defending Calcutta.

As the year neared its end, Hurricanes moved closer to the frontier, where from airstrips constructed in dried-out paddy fields, they gave support to the first faltering British counter-offensive – a push into the Arakan as the western coastal area of Burma was known. One of the Hurricane squadrons involved was No. 136 and in

Robert Jackson's *Hawker Hurricane*, Pilot Officer – later Wing Commander – Gordon Conway describes how:

> January [1943] was a month of intensive operations in which many raids were made by both sides. Later in the month, Group laid on a massive effort to disrupt enemy routes. We flew forward to the strips immediately behind our troops to obtain maximum range, and . . . at dawn, scores of us took off at pre-arranged intervals with orders to shoot up anything military. We attacked and burned up a convoy of petrol bowsers and lorries and came back to base very pleased with the havoc.

Despite such assistance, however, the ground troops were first checked, then counter-attacked from the flank and forced into retreat. By mid-May the attempt was over but it seems that it had worried the Japanese. In particular they were clearly alarmed by the Hurricanes' activities and towards the end of May began a series of heavy assaults on their airfields. It was customary at this time for the Hurricane squadrons to operate in pairs, one such grouping being No. 67 with 136, while another was No. 79 with 135. All these units were to see intensive action as Gordon Conway reveals:

> On the 22nd [May] they hit us with twenty-five bombers at 20,000 feet, escorted by fifteen plus Oscars. Both 67 and ourselves intercepted; 67 claimed two destroyed, two probables and one damaged, while we claimed five destroyed, four probables and three damaged . . . I got into the fighter screen and claimed one destroyed and another probable. A week later the Japs repeated this raid, using fifteen plus bombers at 18,000 feet, with twenty plus fighters at 22,000 feet. [Flying Officer] Joe Edwards was leading, and as he dived on the top fighters, another fighter from a different flight turned on to his tail in front of my flight. I gave this Oscar a long burst of cannon, closing from astern, as he literally fell apart. He seemed to stop in mid-air, his port wheel came down followed by his flaps, and with pieces flying off all around he

174

flicked and spun vertically into the sea, just by the airfield. We claimed five, one and two, while 67 claimed three probables and one damaged. So ended a good month in which our only casualties were two pilots, both of whom escaped with slight injuries . . . In six months we (Nos 136 and 67 Squadrons) had destroyed fourteen enemy aircraft, probably destroyed ten and damaged eighteen for the loss of four pilots. Down south, 79 Squadron had also destroyed seventeen enemy aircraft; 135 Squadron had claimed over twenty, but at the great cost of thirteen of their own pilots.

Though they had thus paid a high price for their successes, the Hurricanes were in fact already supreme in the skies above the Arakan. Nor would this supremacy ever be challenged, for from now onwards the Japanese were increasingly compelled to send any reserves that they might have to counter the American offensives in the Pacific. Moreover, while some Hurricane pilots were grappling with Japanese air raids, others, taking advantage of the enemy's preoccupation, were participating in another Allied offensive of a quite different type.

On the night of 14 February 1943, 3,200 men under Orde Wingate, then a colonel but to be a major general within a year, crossed the Chindwin River to penetrate deep into Japanese territory. The 'Chindits', who took their name from the mythical beast – half lion, half griffin – that guarded Burmese pagodas, depended for their supplies on parachute drops from Allied Dakotas. These in turn relied on the protection of strong escorts of Hurricanes.

Apparently Wingate was more than satisfied with the Hurricanes' efforts. In Terence Kelly's *Hurricane and Spitfire Pilots at War*, Squadron Leader 'Denny' Sharp recalls how, at the time of his second expedition behind enemy lines, the Chindit leader personally requested help from Sharp's No. 11 Squadron:

And it was a job going in and strafing a copse of trees alongside a railway line that went north and south. And I said to him: 'You realise that first thing in the morning when we get there, it'll be around about an hour after daylight and by that time the enemy will either have gone from this copse or it'll be captured by your troops. If we go in there and shoot this copse up, how do we know who's in there?' And he said: 'You don't have to worry. You go in and shoot that copse.' So I said: 'Okay, we'll go in and shoot that copse.' So we took off before first light and I had twelve Hurricanes and we arrived there about three quarters of an hour after taking off and we arrived in the middle of a battle and we could tell it was a battle going on because all these smoke bombs were falling along the railway line. Obviously somebody was holding the railway line against somebody who was attacking the railway line. And we didn't know who was attacking the railway line or who was defending the railway line. And so I was afraid to attack anything. I saw this copse about two kilometres farther up the railway line and about five hundred metres off it and we circled around for ten minutes with this battle still going on and I said: 'The only thing we can do is to take that copse.' So that's what we did. We went down and we fired all our rounds into this bloody copse. You wouldn't believe it. And we went back to Imphal. But I never saw Wingate again. He was killed [in an air crash] about two weeks later.

Presumably Wingate had made sure that his men would not occupy the copse in question and had reason to believe that it would be held by the enemy. This episode does illustrate, however, that while Hurricane pilots could estimate the damage they had inflicted on targets at sea or in the open deserts of North Africa, it was often impossible for them to do so in the jungles of Burma. Consequently the effects of their activities on this front were often only appreciated by the men on the ground.

There would be plenty of opportunities for such appreciation. The immediate achievements of Wingate's first raid were minor, and only two-thirds of his men returned to India, a large proportion of them so ravaged by disease that they were judged unfit for further service. Yet their sacrifices were justified, for Wingate had shown that once supply lines were transferred to the air, British and Indian soldiers could out-fight, outwit and outmanoeuvre the Japanese in the jungle. The news did more to raise morale than anything else before or later.

Moreover the Japanese again reacted with concern to this invasion of their territory. To them it indicated that the Chindwin River was not the secure barrier that they had believed. Instead of standing on the defensive, which would have made them very hard to defeat, they therefore decided to gain a better position. Though both sides would talk of a 'March on Delhi' at different times for propaganda purposes, the enemy in reality intended no more than a preventative seizure of the Imphal plain; indeed their leaders forbade an advance on Dimapur, the major base of Britain's Fourteenth Army, which they could easily have taken, on the grounds that this would be pushing too deeply into India.

At the outset it might admittedly have seemed that Dimapur was well out of Japanese reach, and that even their limited plans were the wildest folly. The Allies were not only aware of their enemy's plans but had a considerable preponderance in manpower, in artillery and in tanks – which could in addition outgun the few the Japanese possessed. Best of all as it turned out, when the Japanese offensive began on the night of 7–8 March 1944, the Allies had total command of the air. Indeed Hurribombers were already attacking the Japanese lines of communication, making strikes on bridges, troop positions and transports on roads, railways and rivers. Two squadrons of Hurricane IIDs with 40mm anti-tank guns had also reached the front, 5 Squadron destroying twenty-seven lorries and fourteen bullock carts on 8 January alone, while No. 20 was credited at the end of six months of operations with having hit 348 strongpoints and 501 sampans.

Yet so great was the Japanese speed of movement through difficult terrain that they caught their opponents by surprise. Covered by strikes from Hurribombers, three Allied divisions retired to Imphal where they were joined by the bulk of a fourth, ferried in by air. Nonetheless on 29 March the outnumbered Japanese were able to cut the road to Dimapur about 30 miles north of Imphal, which enabled them to assault the Imphal plain and its vital aerodromes from all directions.

Fortunately the defenders were saved from worse disaster on the 29th by a Hurricane recce pilot. During the latter part of 1943 the Indian Air Force had begun to receive Hurricane IICs, which eventually came to equip eight squadrons. These operated mainly in the Tactical Reconnaissance role, though they did not hesitate to strafe enemy positions whenever opportunity offered and despite extremely accurate AA fire. During the remainder of the campaign in Burma the IAF Hurricane pilots would fly more than 16,000 missions, lose fifty aircraft and receive forty-four decorations for gallantry.

One of these pilots was Squadron Leader Arjan Singh, CO of 1 Squadron Indian Air Force. In the early evening of 29 March he sighted a Japanese battalion less than 10 miles from Imphal airfield. In the gathering dusk Hurricanes from 1 IAF, from another Tac R squadron, 28 Squadron RAF, and from two Hurribomber units, 34 and 42 Squadrons – thirty-three aircraft in all – took off for the area indicated. Flying very low, they spotted the hostile column with the aid of their landing lights, and routed it, killing, as captured enemy documents later confirmed, fourteen officers and over 200 men. Most of the Hurricanes regained their base before nightfall but one at least made an excellent landing in the dark without the aid of a flarepath.

On 4 April the Japanese also laid siege to the British garrison holding Kohima Ridge, the most vulnerable point on the Imphal-Dimapur road. Thereafter the twin battles of Imphal and Kohima continued unabated, while other enemy forces blocked Fourteenth Army's attempts to advance from Dimapur to their relief. Participants on both sides have compared these struggles to the most brutal battles of the First World War. These comments say very little for the standard of generalship displayed on either side, but they do emphasize the extraordinary tenacity of the soldiers from Britain, India and Japan, who by common consent were worthy of each other.

What turned the battles in favour of the British and Commonwealth troops was Allied air supremacy. Hurricanes were pre-eminent among the supporting squadrons, equipping No. 28 and three IAF Tac R units, No. 5 which had converted to IICs and used them on strafing missions or to escort Allied transports, No. 20 which still had tank-busters, and no less than six Hurribomber squadrons. So effective were the last named that five Wellington bombers were withdrawn from other operations in order to ferry their 250lb weapons to the front line. During April over a million pounds of them rained down on the hapless Japanese infantrymen.

Particularly important were the bombs used against the hill of Nunshigum, rising abruptly from the plain only 6 miles north of Imphal, which the Japanese seized on 6 April; next day, however, they suffered such casualties from Hurribomber attacks that the Allies re-took it with little difficulty. The stubborn enemy captured the hill again on the morning of the 11th, but on the 13th the Hurribombers first blasted it, then strafed it from treetop height, interspersing their strikes with dummy runs to keep the defenders' heads down. Under cover of these raids the British and Commonwealth soldiers renewed their assaults and Nunshigum changed hands once more – for the last time.

That was the nearest the Japanese came to their objective, but they persisted in their attacks on Imphal and were as persistently thwarted. How valuable and how varied were the Hurricanes' contributions to this achievement can be seen from an official publication, *The Campaign in Burma*.[2]

'Hurribombers' became part of the pattern of the assault, strafing bunkers, foxholes and gun positions. Hurricanes spotted for the artillery and reconnoitred for the infantry. They shot up and bombed enemy concentrations, dumps, transport, bridges, river craft and locomotives. One squadron of Hurricanes [No. 5] specialised in picking out Japanese road transport at night by its headlamps. When the Japanese 'blacked-out' and travelled by moonlight the Hurricane pilots trailed them by the shadows the vehicles threw across the road. The monsoon in no way diminished their activity.

Similar aid was given in the area of Kohima where four Hurribomber squadrons flew over 2,200 sorties. It was with the support of Hurribomber attacks that Fourteenth Army was finally able to lift the siege of Kohima Ridge by 20 April, though the Japanese retained neighbouring high ground which still blocked the way to Imphal. So the weary battles of attrition dragged on through May, with the Hurricanes operating at maximum intensity.

By this time the pattern first laid down in North Africa, whereby the Army and the Air Force constituted 'one fighting machine', had been adopted on the India–Burma front as well. Pilots would visit brigades detailed for an attack so as to assess the best ways in which they could assist this, while any squadrons not given specific tasks were allocated to a unit called the Army Air Support Control to which the forward ground troops could radio direct requests for assistance as needed. The importance of the Hurricanes in this connection again enjoys official recognition in the Despatch of Air Chief Marshal Sir Richard Peirse, the Allied Air Commander-in-Chief:

> The enemy's efforts to deploy in the Imphal plain during May 1944 were decisively defeated by Hurricane attacks at short intervals on any concentrations reported by ground troops through our Army Air Support Control operating at a high level of efficiency.

One Hurribomber attack on 18 May in the neighbourhood of Kohima was witnessed by Major Elliott of the 7th Battalion, the Worcestershire Regiment, who considered it:

> The most frightening thing . . . experienced so far . . . The target was only a hundred and seventy yards away, so the pilots were releasing their bombs right over our heads, which gave us the impression that they would drop into our trenches, instead of swishing low overhead on to the enemy bunkers.[3]

Happily only the enemy bunkers were harmed.

Also on 18 May the monsoon broke. This may have 'in no way diminished' the Hurricanes' activity, but it wrecked the already perilous Japanese supply lines. Nonetheless their commanders would still not withdraw. It was not until 22 June that relief forces broke through to Imphal and only in early July that a general retirement was ordered. This refusal to face facts merely ensured that Japanese casualties would be too great ever to be made good. From this moment they could not hope to do more than delay the Allied reconquest of Burma.

Indeed it might be wondered whether it was really necessary for the Allies to reconquer Burma at all. In October 1944 the titanic Battle of Leyte Gulf, the largest naval battle in history, all but annihilated the Japanese fleet and ensured the loss of the Philippines, which in turn would cut off the Japanese from their captured territories to the south and the natural resources for which they had gone to war in the first place. Their final defeat was thus certain and would in no way be affected by Britain's expenditure of money, materials and, most important, men's lives in liberating Burma. Perhaps it was hoped that this would belatedly restore British prestige; if so the hope proved vain, for soon after the war Burma would not only cease to be a British possession but would leave the Commonwealth altogether.

Not of course that these considerations reflect on the brilliance of the Hurricanes' part in Burma's reconquest. The variety of their duties was as great as ever. They carried out reconnaissance missions including one on 13 November by one of Bomber Command's most famous pilots, Group Captain Leonard Cheshire VC, who, it should be noted, had never flown a Hurricane before. They attacked bridges, transport and supply dumps. Six squadrons of them even took time off combat duties to spray DDT over the road south through the Kabaw Valley, reputedly the most highly malarial spot on earth, thereby reducing the casualties caused by disease to a lower level than anyone had considered possible.

Yet the main task of the Hurricane pilots was still to provide close support to the advancing armies. By the end of October the number of pounds of bombs launched by Hurribombers had risen to five and a half million. Again and again they played a major part in the seizure of enemy positions. On 18 October Tiddim was captured after fighter-bombers had dived through the early morning mist to make an attack which, in addition to the damage it caused, masked the noise of tanks moving up to the assault. 'Vital Corner' fell on 2 November 1944 after a raid by four squadrons of Hurribombers; Kennedy Peak on 4 November after Hurribombers had destroyed three Japanese bunkers; Gangaw on 10 January 1945 after they had hit five bunkers out of six.

Nor were the Hurricanes only using bombs, for in November

1944 20 Squadron received Mark IVs to supplement its IIDs. They were armed not only with anti-tank guns but with rockets, and on 20 January 1945 seven of the squadron's pilots attacked Japanese defences at Monywa with the latter weapons. Lieutenant Colonel Taunton, commanding the 1st Battalion, the Northamptonshire Regiment, was among those who witnessed their assault:

> All aircraft peeled off from a left-hand circle and dived down over my head on to the target . . . Two things impressed me as a casual observer. I leave it to the readers of this report to decide for themselves what impression the Japanese garrison of some 30 or 40 had of the venomous roar of the discharge of the rockets and the speed at which they travelled and the great accuracy and earthquake effect which followed each rocket strike.[4]

20 Squadron would enjoy a still more important success on 19 February. A week earlier Fourteenth Army had crossed the Irrawaddy River at Myinmu as a preliminary to an advance on Mandalay, and Flight Lieutenants Farquharson and Ballard were out looking for Japanese armour reported to be moving towards the bridgehead, when they sighted what appeared to be a small shed. When fired upon, however, this turned out to be a cleverly camouflaged tank – which the pilots promptly destroyed. Soon afterwards they destroyed a second one; then, finding further targets, they called up the rest of their squadron which reduced eleven more tanks to blazing wreckage.

This action proved the overture to a series of strikes by Hurribombers and tank-busters which, after a month of savage encounters, resulted in the capture of Mandalay. The shattered Japanese retreated eastwards, so leaving the road to Rangoon wide open for Fourteenth Army. The soldiers set off in a spectacular dash southwards – though ironically they did not have the satisfaction of taking the Burmese capital, for this was occupied instead as the result of a seaborne landing on 3 May.

Above this final advance, the Hurricanes, moving forward to new airfields as these were lost to the Japanese, fell on enemy transport with unabated determination. Francis K. Mason in *The*

Hawker Hurricane has again found an admirable extract from a Squadron Diary – that of 20 Squadron – which typifies their exploits:

On 13 April, 1945, the squadron began operations from Thedaw airfield in partnership with No. 28 Tactical Reconnaissance Squadron, also with Hurricanes. For the first few days the taxi strip was used (for take-off) until the engineers, with the aid of 3,000 coolies, completed repairs on the bomb-damaged main runway. The eastern sector, in the Heho area, provided the squadron with a happy hunting ground, the game being mostly motor transport. To the south army air support was given to the 5th Division in its rapid advance on Rangoon via Pyinmana and Toungoo. South of Pyinmana a Japanese convoy of about 40 vehicles was caught trying to make a dash for it. However timely intervention by the squadron accounted for 17 flamers and many damaged; discouraging to say the least for the Japanese troops in the area. To the west, river craft, pontoons, rafts, etc, on the Irrawaddy came in for the squadron's attention and many successful strikes were made in this area.

Within two weeks our forward troops in the south had advanced beyond our Hurricanes' range. It was therefore decided to move the squadron to Tennant airstrip at Toungoo, whence Pegu and the Sittang ferry – the main escape route from Burma – would be within our range. The squadron, with the minimum of kit, landed at Tennant on the 28th. In spite of various discomforts experienced at our new location, and what appeared to be colossal administrative disorganization, the squadron became operational immediately and was rewarded with excellent targets in the Pegu area. It became apparent that the Japanese intended to retreat from Pegu and cross the Sittang by ferry and, as a result, presented the Hurricane IIDs and IVs with ideal targets. The Mark IVs concentrated on the river craft and pontoons on the Sittang while the IIDs dealt with the resulting bottleneck of motor transport on the road leading to the west bank of the ferry. At the end of one day (30

April) the squadron had accounted for 46 flamers and very many vehicles damaged.

During the summer most of the RAF squadrons replaced their Hurricanes with more modern aircraft, chiefly American Thunderbolts, but when in early August weapons vastly more deadly and horrible than any the Hurricanes carried fell on two Japanese cities, the Hawker fighter still provided the equipment of No. 20, No. 28 and the eight Indian Air Force Tac R squadrons. The RAF Official History thus summarizes its achievements in Burma:

Everywhere the ubiquitous Hurricane was to be seen.

NOTES
1 Volume III: *The Fight is Won.*
2 This was prepared for South East Asia Command by the Central Office of Information. It was written by Lieutenant Colonel Frank Owen, editor of the theatre newspaper *Seac.*
3 Quoted in *Kohima* by Arthur Swinson, who himself served in the battle.
4 Quoted in *Hawker Hurricane* by Bruce Robertson and Gerald Scarborough. In this Mr Robertson details the history of the Hurricane, while Mr Scarborough describes how to prepare scale models of various versions of an aircraft which for him 'has long been a pet subject'.

Chapter 14

Assessment

From 3 September 1939, when Britain declared war on Germany, to 2 September 1945, when Japanese representatives signed the formal document of surrender on board the American battleship *Missouri* in Tokyo Bay, there was not a day when there were no Hurricanes in the front line; but once the war was over they disappeared with almost stunning rapidity. The last Hurricane squadron in the RAF, No. 6, completed its conversion to Hawker Tempests on 15 January 1947 and Hurricanes remained on active service with the air forces of Ireland, India, Portugal and Persia for only a little longer.

Not that this really mattered, for the Hurricane had done more than enough to secure its reputation while the war was being fought. No other aircraft had participated in so many campaigns or carried out so many different duties in such varied conditions. When seeking the reasons for its success, Dr John W. Fozard, in *Sydney Camm and the Hurricane*, tells us that:

In my view it resided in the aircraft's TIMING, in its PERFORMANCE (not outstanding but more-than-adequate), in its FLYING QUALITIES (pilot-friendly, as we say today, and making it one of the best armament platforms of WW2), in its EASE OF PRODUCTION and hence its RAPIDITY OF REPAIR and RUGGEDNESS IN SERVICE together with its continued ADAPTABILITY TO DIFFERENT ROLES in ever-changing theatres of battle.

For all these assets and qualities, and the consequences that stemmed from them in the factories and in service around the world, the Hurricane rightly can be termed immortal and the achievements of Camm and his team deservedly lauded.

But what did the pilots think of it? For the Hurricane as an interceptor, we can turn to Wing Commander Roland Beamont who had immense experience of flying fighter aircraft either in combat or as a test pilot. In *Phoenix into Ashes* he declares:

No pilot who ever flew into a 'beehive' of Junkers, Dorniers or Heinkels with their escorting fighters, or took off through snow or smog on a night patrol or, faced with a night landing with vision reduced in mist to one or two vague flares and holding the glide steady at 80 mph, waited for the first bounce and then landed safely off it – none of these will ever forget the confidence we had in our Hurricanes.

For the Hurricane as a fighter-bomber, there can be no more suitable witness than Wing Commander Denys Gillam whom Douglas Bader calls 'the unrivalled maestro of the low-level attack'. In Bader's *Fight for the Sky*, Gillam says of the Hurricane:

It was the finest gun-platform of them all. It also took a staggering amount of punishment and still managed to get home. I have seen pilots bring them back with most of the fin and rudder missing; with a hole in the wing where a Bofors shell had penetrated and taken out the complete ammunition box; indeed any pilot in a Hurricane squadron will recall the extraordinary amount of damage this fighter could absorb and still keep flying.

Both Beamont and Gillam had 'good' wars, at least while serving on Hurricane squadrons. The same could not be said of Pilot Officer Pat Wells of 249 Squadron on 28 November 1940, for on this date his Hurricane was attacked by the German 'ace' Adolf Galland who later reported that Wells was 'dead by burning'.

Happily he was wrong. The Hurricane remained airborne just

long enough for Wells to escape by parachute and although he was badly burned he made a full recovery, was flying again within three months and finished the war as a squadron leader. In *Hawker Hurricane* by Peter Jacobs he pays this tribute:

> The Hurricane was built in several marks, some of which little is known of, and took part in air battles on every front, even the Battle of the Atlantic from the end of a catapult. It seems that every operational task was possible in a Hurricane and I believe that had the radiator not been where it was then she could have successfully carried a torpedo!
>
> My first flight was in June 1940 . . . and [I] went on to complete nearly 300 operations on Mark Is and IIs; these included the Battle of Britain, fighter sweeps over northern France, flying off HMS *Ark Royal* for service in Malta and then on to North Africa for the war in the desert. My final flight was from Malta back to Tunisia after attacking searchlights in Sicily which were causing problems to the airborne forces during that invasion.
>
> An exceptionally sturdy aircraft, the Hurricane never let me down (except from battle damage) and how my aircraft stayed together after Adolf Galland's assault on me in 1940, with 132 machine-gun rounds and 64 cannon shells, is a mystery to me. Incidentally, I only ever had one mid-air collision. Whilst flying a Curtiss Mohawk at an OTU [Operational Training Unit] in the Middle East, a pupil flying a Hurricane collided with me; the Mohawk was a wreck, but the Hurricane went on to complete the exercise!

The final judgement though must be left to Group Captain Peter Townsend in *Duel of Eagles*, because it not only shows the worth of the aircraft but, impliedly, that of the men who flew it as well:

> We ourselves thought the Hurricane was great, and we proved it.

Index

Note: The ranks of the service personnel are those held at the time of the incident or incidents described.

189